Grace Uncovered: A Commentary on Romans 8

Lawrence Muigai

Published by Lawrence Muigai, 2024.

While every precaution has been taken in the preparation of this book, the publisher assumes no responsibility for errors or omissions, or for damages resulting from the use of the information contained herein.

GRACE UNCOVERED: A COMMENTARY ON ROMANS 8

First edition. June 17, 2024.

ISBN: 979-8227554215

Written by Lawrence Muigai.

Also by Lawrence Muigai

Unmasking the Shadows
Unmasking the Shadows

Standalone
Grace Uncovered: A Commentary on Romans 8

Watch for more at https://greceandtruth.blogspot.com/.

Table of Contents

Dedication:

To Pastor Martin, my guide through the maze of scripture and the beacon of light that led me to the path of salvation life. Your wisdom, patience, and unwavering faith have been a source of strength and inspiration to me throughout my journey of faith. Though you taught the word of God with all your heart and knowledge, it is my deepest desire that this book opens new horizons for you, revealing the boundless depths of God's grace that surpasses all works-based piety. May this dedication be a token of my gratitude for your invaluable mentorship and a testament to the transformative power of grace.

To my childhood friend, Bonnie Kim, who shared in the trials and triumphs of our upbringing, rising above the limitations imposed by our circumstances. Together, we defied the odds, proving that our worth is not defined by societal labels or economic status. As I dedicate this book to you, Bonnie, I offer it as a gift of hope and possibility—a testament to the limitless potential that lies within each of us to know God in a new dimension. May this book serve as a beacon of light in your life, illuminating the path to a deeper understanding of God's love and grace.

This book is dedicated to Pastor Martin and Bonnie Kim, two souls whose presence in my life has left an indelible mark on my heart. May it be a source of inspiration and revelation to you both, as you continue to journey in faith and discover the unfathomable riches of God's grace.

Preface:

Welcome to "Grace Uncovered," a journey into the heart of God's grace—a grace that defies human logic, transcends religious legalism, and transforms lives with its boundless love and mercy. As you embark on this exploration with me, allow me to share the story behind the genesis of this book and the fervent passion that drives its message.

For much of my life, I grappled with the weight of uncertainty and fear, haunted by the belief that my salvation hinged on my ability to shun the wrong and do the right. I lived under the shadow of doubt, never quite sure if my actions were enough to secure my place in heaven. Amidst the turmoil of my soul, a certain preacher's words pierced through my despair, painting a grim picture of judgment and condemnation that left me feeling utterly hopeless.

In the depths of my despair, I stumbled upon the message of grace—a message so radical, so transformative, that it seemed almost too good to be true. And yet, as I delved into the pages of Romans, I discovered that grace was not merely a concept but the very essence of salvation itself. Romans, often viewed as the executive summary of the entire epistle, serves as a powerful testament to the life-changing power of grace—a grace that extends from the moment of salvation to every aspect of the believer's journey.

In "Grace Uncovered," I invite you to journey with me through the corridors of Romans, as we uncover the profound truths that lie hidden within its pages. Together, we will explore the doctrines of substitution, salvation, federal representation, sanctification, adoption, and more, each one shedding light on the unfathomable depths of God's grace.

But more than just an intellectual pursuit, "Grace Uncovered" is an invitation to a deeper relationship with God. It is a call to move beyond mere knowledge and into a profound experience of His love and presence in our lives. As you journey through these pages, may you be challenged, inspired, and transformed by the boundless grace of God that knows no limits and exceeds all expectations.

So join me, dear reader, as we uncover the grace that changes everything—a grace that is more than enough to save, to transform, and to bring us into the fullness of life in Christ. And may your heart be forever changed by the revelation of God's grace, as we embark on this journey together.

Acknowledgments:

In the tapestry of life, there are threads of grace woven intricately throughout, guiding our paths and illuminating our journey. As I reflect on the journey that led me to write this book, "Grace Uncovered," I am overwhelmed with gratitude for the individuals whose influence and support have shaped my understanding of grace and fueled my passion for sharing its message with others.

First and foremost, I extend my heartfelt appreciation to Pastor Macharia of Christian Outreach Ministries, whose ministry became a beacon of hope in a time when I was hiding away from my guilty self. It was by God's divine design that our paths crossed, replacing fear with hope and confidence in the boundless grace of our Savior. Every bus fare I paid to attend your church was an investment in my spiritual growth, and your tender and fatherly shepherdship will forever be etched in my heart.

I also want to acknowledge Pastor Anthony Ndung'u, whose big heart and relentless dedication to nurturing my faith have left an indelible mark on my life. From the countless hours spent studying the Word together to the selfless act of lending me his computer to write this book, your generosity knows no bounds. It is a testament to your character and unwavering commitment to the Kingdom of God. You will always hold a special place in my heart, and I am forever grateful for your friendship and mentorship.

To Pastor Macharia, Pastor Anthony, and all those who have poured into my life with love, wisdom, and encouragement, I offer my deepest gratitude. Your support has been instrumental in shaping the message of grace that I am privileged to share with the world through this book. May God bless you abundantly for your faithfulness and may the seeds you have sown continue to bear fruit for His Kingdom.

Foreword:

As I stand at the threshold of introducing you to "Grace Uncovered," I am reminded of the winding path that has led me to this moment—a journey marked by moments of doubt, discovery, and divine intervention. It is with a sense of awe and gratitude that I offer this book to you, dear reader, as a testament to the transformative power of God's grace in my own life and as an invitation to embark on a journey of discovery and transformation.

For much of my life, I grappled with the complexities of faith, wrestling with questions of identity, purpose, and salvation. Raised in a religious environment that emphasized works-based piety, I found myself trapped in a cycle of fear and uncertainty, unsure if my actions were ever enough to earn God's favor. It was in the midst of this turmoil that I encountered the message of grace—a message so radical, so liberating, that it shook the foundations of my faith and set me on a path of rediscovery.

Through the pages of Romans, I discovered a treasure trove of truth that illuminated the pathway to salvation by grace alone through faith alone in Christ alone. It was as if the words of Scripture leapt off the page, breathing new life into my weary soul and filling me with a sense of hope and assurance that I had never known before. In Romans, I found not just an intellectual exercise but a roadmap for living—a blueprint for navigating the complexities of faith and experiencing the fullness of life in Christ.

"Grace Uncovered" is the culmination of my journey—a testament to the grace that has sustained me, transformed me, and set me free. In its pages, you will find not just a theological treatise but a journey of the heart—a journey that invites you to explore the depths of God's love and the boundless riches of His grace. From salvation to sanctification, from adoption to the indwelling Spirit, each chapter is a reflection of the profound truths that have reshaped my understanding of God and His purposes for my life.

As you embark on this journey with me, may you be challenged, inspired, and transformed by the message of grace that lies at the heart of "Grace Uncovered." May you come to know, as I have, the immeasurable depths of God's love and the inexhaustible riches of His grace. And may you be empowered to live a life that bears witness to the transformative power of the gospel, shining brightly in a world that desperately needs the light of Christ.

With deepest gratitude and anticipation,

Lawrence Njihia

`1 Introduction:

Welcome to "Grace Uncovered," a journey through the profound truths and transformative power of God's grace, as revealed in the epistle to the Romans. In this exploration, we delve deep into the heart of Paul's letter, particularly focusing on the pivotal chapter 8, which serves as an executive summary of the gospel of grace.

Romans 8 encapsulates the essence of salvation by grace, offering a comprehensive framework for understanding the foundational doctrines of Christianity. As we unravel the layers of Paul's message, we will discover that this chapter serves as a beacon of hope, illuminating the path to redemption and liberation from the bondage of sin.

Throughout "Grace Uncovered," readers will be equipped to grapple with the profound theological questions surrounding grace, salvation, and the nature of God's unmerited favor. By delving into the depths of Romans, we will confront the complexities of human nature, the sovereignty of God, and the unfathomable depths of His love.

This book is not merely an academic exercise; it is a journey of faith, inviting readers to engage with the timeless truths of Scripture and to experience firsthand the life-changing power of grace. Through reflection, study, and prayerful contemplation, readers will be empowered to navigate the complexities of their own spiritual journey and to embrace the liberating truth of God's grace.

So join us on this exploration of "Grace Uncovered," as we embark on a quest to unravel the mysteries of salvation, deepen our understanding of God's grace, and embark on a transformative journey of faith. Let us journey together, guided by the timeless wisdom of Scripture and the illuminating power of God's grace.

Romans 8:1:

As we step into the opening verse of Romans 8, we are met with a declaration of profound significance, a declaration that reverberates through the corridors of time and echoes into the depths of our souls. It is a declaration that beckons us to the very heart of the gospel, inviting us to behold the wondrous truth that lies at its core.

In these few words, Paul unveils a truth of staggering magnitude, a truth that has the power to transform lives and reshape destinies. He declares boldly and unequivocally: "There is therefore now no condemnation for those who are in Christ Jesus."

With this declaration, Paul sets the stage for a journey of discovery, a journey into the heart of God's grace and mercy. He invites us to explore the depths of what it means to be "in Christ Jesus," to understand the profound implications of our union with Him.

But perhaps what is most striking about this declaration is not just what it affirms, but also what it negates. In a world fraught with judgment and condemnation, Paul's words offer a message of liberation and hope. They declare that for those who are in Christ Jesus, there is no condemnation—not now, not ever.

As we embark on our study of Romans 8:1, let us come with open hearts and minds, ready to encounter the truth that sets us free. Let us allow ourselves to be drawn deeper into the mystery of God's grace, as we seek to understand how this truth about no condemnation has come to be.

May this exploration awaken within us a hunger for righteousness and a thirst for the living water of God's word. And may it leave us yearning to delve further into the riches of His grace, as we seek to know Him more deeply and to walk in the freedom that He has so graciously bestowed upon us.

Nolle Prosequi

In Romans 8:1, Paul declares a profound truth that resonates with believers throughout history: "There is therefore now no condemnation for those who are in Christ Jesus." This declaration echoes the concept of "nolle prosequi" or "no prosecution," a legal term indicating the decision of a prosecutor to drop charges against a defendant.

In some jurisdictions, a president or a chief executive possesses the power to grant nolle prosequi, effectively ending legal proceedings against an individual. Similarly, in certain legal systems, a judge holds the power of veto, allowing them to halt or overturn a verdict.

However, the parallel drawn here is limited, for the sovereignty of God surpasses any human authority. God is not just a ruler or a judge; He is the righteous judge of the entire universe. His judgments are perfect and just, untainted by human fallibility or bias.

What makes this declaration in Romans 8:1 even more profound is the basis upon which it rests. It's not merely a decision of amnesty or pardon granted by a human authority. Instead, it is rooted in the redemptive work of Christ on the cross.

Throughout the New Testament, we encounter numerous passages that affirm this truth. In John 3:16, we learn that God so loved the world that He gave His only Son, that whoever believes in Him should not perish but have eternal life. In Romans 5:8, Paul writes that God demonstrates His love for us in that while we were still sinners, Christ died for us.

The Old Testament also foreshadows this reality. Isaiah 53:5 prophesies about the suffering of the Messiah, saying, "But he was pierced for our transgressions; he was crushed for our iniquities; upon him was the chastisement that brought us peace, and with his wounds, we are healed."

Therefore, when Paul declares "no condemnation" in Romans 8:1, he is affirming the foundational truth of the gospel: Christ has paid the penalty for our sins in full. As a result, those who are in Christ Jesus are no longer under condemnation. It's not that our sins are overlooked or ignored; rather, they are fully atoned for by the sacrificial death of Jesus Christ.

In light of this, we can confidently assert that we have no case to answer before the divine court. The righteousness of Christ has been imputed to us, and we stand justified before God. This truth should fill us with gratitude and awe, inspiring us to live lives that reflect the grace and mercy we have received.

God: The Justifier Of The Ungodly

In delving into the subtopic of "God the Justifier of the Ungodly," we encounter a profound theological truth that lies at the heart of the gospel message. This truth challenges conventional human notions of justice and righteousness, revealing the depth of God's grace and mercy towards sinful humanity.

At the core of this concept is the recognition that God justifies the ungodly—not based on their own merits or works of righteousness, but solely through faith in the redemptive work of Jesus Christ. This radical notion stands in stark contrast to human systems of justice, where guilt is often determined by one's actions and deeds.

Scripture resounds with the testimony of God's grace towards the ungodly. In Romans 4:5, Paul declares, "And to the one who does not work but believes in him who justifies the ungodly, his faith is counted as righteousness." Here, Paul emphasizes that it is faith, not works, that brings about justification before God.

The epitome of this truth is found in the person of Jesus Christ, who offered up his own righteousness on behalf of the unrighteous. 2 Corinthians 5:21 encapsulates this reality: "For our sake he made him to be sin who knew no sin, so that in him we might become the righteousness of God." Through the sacrificial death of Christ, God reconciles sinful humanity to Himself, imputing His righteousness to those who believe in Him.

This justification is not a one-time event but encompasses the entirety of a believer's life—past, present, and future sins. Hebrews 10:14 affirms this truth, stating, "For by a single offering he has perfected for all time those who are being sanctified." Through Christ's atoning sacrifice, believers are declared righteous in God's sight, freed from the burden of striving to keep the requirements of the law.

As a result, the righteous judge brings down His gavel and pronounces believers acquitted and justified. Romans 8:33-34 proclaims, "Who shall bring any charge against God's elect? It is God who justifies. Who is to condemn? Christ Jesus is the one who died—more than that, who was raised—who is at the right hand of God, who indeed is interceding for us." In Christ, believers receive a clean slate, absolved of guilt and condemnation.

The truth of God justifying the ungodly through faith in Jesus Christ shatters human conceptions of justice and righteousness. It is a testament to the depth of God's grace and the sufficiency of Christ's sacrifice on behalf of sinful humanity. May we embrace this truth with humble gratitude, recognizing that our righteousness is found solely in Him.

In Adam Or In Christ?

Here we delve into the profound theological concept of federal representation, highlighting the contrast between humanity's spiritual condition in Adam, the representative head of the fallen race, and in Christ, the representative head of the redeemed.

In Adam, all humanity is imputed with his sin and its consequences. This concept finds its roots in the biblical narrative of Adam and Eve's disobedience in the Garden of Eden, resulting in the fall of humanity into sin. Romans 5:12 succinctly articulates this truth: "Therefore, just as sin came into the world through one man, and death through sin, and so death spread to all men because all sinned." In Adam, all are considered sinners, not based on their individual actions, but by virtue of their union with him as their federal head.

Conversely, in Christ, believers are imputed with His righteousness and find favor with God on account of His redemptive work. 2 Corinthians 5:21 encapsulates this truth: "For our sake he made him to be sin who knew no sin, so that in him we might become the righteousness of God." Through faith in Christ, believers are united with Him and receive the benefits of His righteousness, irrespective of their conduct or adherence to the law.

This contrast between Adam and Christ underscores the importance of spiritual union and identity. Those who remain "in Adam" are spiritually dead and separated from God due to sin, while those who are "in Christ" are made alive and reconciled to God through His righteousness.

This truth is further elaborated in Paul's writings, particularly in Romans 6:23: "For the wages of sin is death, but the free gift of God is eternal life in Christ Jesus our Lord." Here, Paul contrasts the consequences of being "in Adam" (death) with the gift of eternal life bestowed upon those who are "in Christ."

The concept of being "in Adam or in Christ" highlights the foundational truth of federal representation in Scripture. Through Adam, all are imputed with sin and its consequences, while through Christ, believers are imputed with righteousness and receive the gift of eternal life. This profound reality underscores the significance of spiritual union with Christ and the transformative power of His redemptive work in the lives of believers.

Romans 8:2

In Romans 8:2, Paul introduces a powerful analogy that illustrates the transformative power of the Spirit in the lives of believers. He contrasts two laws: "the law of the Spirit of life in Christ Jesus" and "the law of sin and of death." This juxtaposition mirrors the principles governing flight, drawing a parallel between the aerodynamic forces that lift an airplane above the law of gravity and the spiritual dynamics that liberate believers from the law of sin and death.

Just as the principles of aerodynamics enable an airplane to overcome the force of gravity and soar through the skies, so too does the law of the Spirit of life in Christ Jesus set believers free from the gravitational pull of sin and death. This analogy captures the essence of the believer's liberation through the indwelling presence of the Holy Spirit, who imparts spiritual life and power.

The concept of aerodynamics or Bernoulli's principle exemplifies how understanding and harnessing natural laws can lead to freedom from physical constraints. Similarly, embracing the spiritual principles revealed in Christ enables believers to transcend the spiritual bondage of sin and death.

This analogy serves as a precursor to the subsequent exploration of the subtopics within Romans 8, where Paul further elaborates on the implications of living according to the Spirit versus living according to the flesh. Just as an airplane must operate within the parameters of aerodynamic principles to maintain flight, believers are called to walk in accordance with the law of the Spirit, experiencing the fullness of life and freedom found in Christ.

The Law And The Curse

Under this head, we confront the sobering reality of humanity's inherited nature from Adam and the consequences of living under the law without the empowerment of the Spirit.

Scripture teaches that through Adam's disobedience, sin entered the world, and humanity inherited a sinful nature (Romans 5:12). This inherited nature predisposes humanity to rebellion against God and renders them spiritually dead (Ephesians 2:1). As a result, apart from Christ, all are under the curse of sin and death (Galatians 3:10).

The law, though spiritual, exposes the depth of humanity's sinfulness and incapacity to fulfill its righteous requirements. Romans 7:14 reveals, "For we know that the law is spiritual, but I am of the flesh, sold under sin." Here, Paul acknowledges the inherent conflict between the spiritual nature of the law and humanity's fallen, carnal state.

Furthermore, the unregenerate person is enslaved to sin, unable to free themselves from its grip. Romans 6:16 illustrates this bondage, stating, "Do you not know that if you present yourselves to anyone as obedient slaves, you are slaves of the one whom you obey, either of sin, which leads to death, or of obedience, which leads to righteousness?"

The law demands perfect obedience, requiring adherence to its precepts without fail. However, due to humanity's fallen nature, no one can keep the law perfectly (Romans 3:23). As a result, all are declared under a curse, for "cursed be everyone who does not abide by all things written in the Book of the Law, and do them" (Galatians 3:10).

All in all, scripture underscores humanity's desperate plight apart from Christ. Inherited sin nature and enslavement to sin render humanity incapable of meeting the righteous demands of the law. As a result, all are under the curse of sin and death. It is only through the redemptive work of Christ and the empowering presence of the Spirit that believers are liberated from this curse and granted the gift of spiritual life and freedom in Christ (Galatians 3:13-14).

Grace The Principle Of Life

Still in Romans 8:2, we encounter the transformative power of God's grace as the principle that bestows life and righteousness upon believers.

At the heart of this concept lies the recognition of God's inherent power and sovereignty. While humanity is powerless to save itself or attain righteousness through its own efforts, God intervenes with His grace. Ephesians 2:8-9 encapsulates this truth: "For by grace you have been saved through faith. And this is not your own doing; it is the gift of God, not a result of works, so that no one may boast." Salvation and righteousness are gifts freely given by God, not earned through human merit or effort.

Relationship with God is not based on human achievement or performance, but on God's redemptive work on behalf of humanity. Romans 3:24 declares, "and are justified by his grace as a gift, through the redemption that is in Christ Jesus." Through Christ's sacrificial death and resurrection, God extends His grace to humanity, offering forgiveness and reconciliation.

In His redemptive work, God imputes His own righteousness to believers in place of their unrighteousness. 2 Corinthians 5:21 reaffirms this truth: "For our sake he made him to be sin who knew no sin, so that in him we might become the righteousness of God." Through faith in Christ, believers are clothed in His righteousness, standing blameless before God.

The conclusion drawn from this truth is clear: Christ is the only source of life and a right standing with God. John 14:6 emphasizes this exclusivity, with Jesus declaring, "I am the way, and the truth, and the life. No one comes to the Father except through me." Apart from Christ, there is no access to God or eternal life.

The centrality of God's grace in the salvation and righteousness of believers can not be over-stressed. It is through His grace alone that humanity finds forgiveness, reconciliation, and new life in Christ. May we humbly receive and embrace this grace, recognizing Christ as the sole source of life and righteousness.

Redeemed From The Curse

Still under Romans 8:2, we confront the hopeless situation humanity faced under the law and the redemptive work of Christ that liberated believers from this bondage.

Before the coming of Christ, humanity found itself in a desperate predicament under the law. Galatians 3:10 highlights this reality: "For all who rely on works of the law are under a curse; for it is written, 'Cursed be everyone who does not abide by all things written in the Book of the Law, and do them.'" Despite earnest efforts to adhere to the written code, humanity consistently fell short, unable to please God through their own righteousness.

However, in His mercy and love, God intervened to redeem humanity from the curse of the law. Galatians 4:4-5 proclaims, "But when the fullness of time had come, God sent forth his Son, born of woman, born under the law, to redeem those who were under the law, so that we might receive adoption as sons." Through the incarnation of Jesus Christ, God entered into human history to fulfill the righteous requirements of the law on behalf of humanity.

Christ's obedience to the law culminated in His ultimate act of obedience: His sacrificial death on the cross. Philippians 2:8 describes Christ's obedience unto death, stating, "And being found in human form, he humbled himself by becoming obedient to the point of death, even death on a cross." Through His death, Christ atoned for the sins of humanity, bearing the curse of the law in our place.

As a result of Christ's obedience, believers are imputed with right standing before God. Galatians 3:13-14 declares, "Christ redeemed us from the curse of the law by becoming a curse for us—for it is written, 'Cursed is everyone who is hanged on a tree'—so that in Christ Jesus the blessing of Abraham might come to the Gentiles, so that we might receive the promised Spirit through faith." Through faith in Christ's death and resurrection, believers are united with Him in His death and resurrection, experiencing newness of life and receiving the blessings promised to Abraham.

It's clear how the Spirit of God, through scriptures illuminates the transformative power of Christ's redemptive work in liberating believers from the bondage of the law. Through His obedience unto death, believers are redeemed, justified, and blessed, receiving the promised Spirit through faith in Christ. May we embrace this truth with gratitude and live in the freedom and blessings secured for us by Christ's sacrifice.

The Letter Killeth

Here, we delve into the concept of spiritual death as separation from God and the role of the law in exacerbating humanity's sinful condition.

Death, in its spiritual sense, represents separation from God—the source of life and righteousness. When Adam, the first man, transgressed the single commandment given to him by God, he became alienated from God, experiencing spiritual death (Genesis 3:6-7). This separation from God resulted in the pervasive presence of sin and death in humanity.

The apostle Paul elucidates this truth in Romans 7:9-11: "I was once alive apart from the law, but when the commandment came, sin came alive and I died. The very commandment that promised life proved to be death to me. For sin, seizing an opportunity through the commandment, deceived me and through it killed me." Here, Paul reflects on his own experience to illustrate the lethal power of the law in exposing and exacerbating human sinfulness.

The law, though holy and righteous, serves to reveal the true nature of humanity's sinfulness. Romans 7:7 affirms this truth: "What then shall we say? That the law is sin? By no means! Yet if it had not been for the law, I would not have known sin. For I would not have known what it is to covet if the law had not said, 'You shall not covet.'" The law unveils the depth of humanity's depravity and the extent of its need for redemption.

Paradoxically, the law, which was intended to give life, ends up bringing death to humanity. Romans 7:10 declares, "The very commandment that promised life proved to be death to me." The law, by revealing the multitude of ways in which humanity falls short of God's standards, exacerbates humanity's sinful condition, leading to death.

Ultimately, the wages of sin are death (Romans 6:23), highlighting the dire consequences of living in rebellion against God's righteous standards. Apart from Christ, humanity remains under the condemnation of the law, facing the inevitable consequence of spiritual and eternal death.

The lethal power of the law exposes and exacerbates human sinfulness. It serves as a sobering reminder of humanity's desperate need for redemption and salvation, which can only be found in Christ, who liberates believers from the bondage of sin and death. May we humbly recognize our need for Christ's redemptive work and embrace the life-giving grace offered through Him.

Romans 8:3:

As we journey through the depths of Romans 8, we encounter a profound truth that unveils the essence of our redemption in Christ. In verse 3, the apostle Paul presents us with a pivotal revelation—one that sheds light on the inadequacy of the law and the transformative power of Christ's redemptive work. This verse beckons us to explore the intricacies of our salvation, inviting us to delve deeper into subsequent subtopics that illuminate its profound implications in our lives.

In a world characterized by striving and performance-based righteousness, the message of verse 3 comes as a liberating truth. It reminds us that our righteousness cannot be attained through adherence to the law, for the law, though holy and righteous, is powerless to save us. Instead, our redemption is found solely in Christ, who came in the likeness of sinful flesh to condemn sin in the flesh.

As we embark on this exploration, we are invited to consider the significance of Christ's incarnation—the divine taking on human form—in fulfilling the righteous requirements of the law on our behalf. We are called to contemplate the sacrificial aspect of His death on the cross, through which sin was condemned, and victory over sin and death was secured for believers.

Moreover, verse 3 challenges us to reflect on our identification with Christ and the newness of life that we experience through union with Him. It prompts us to contrast the law, which brings condemnation, with the grace and salvation offered through faith in Christ.

As we delve into the subtopics that illuminate the truth of verse 3, may we be enriched with a deeper understanding of our redemption in Christ. May this exploration not only inform our minds but also transform our hearts, leading us to live in the fullness of the freedom and victory secured for us by Christ's redemptive work.

The Incarnation Of Christ

In Romans 8:3, the apostle Paul introduces us to the profound concept of the incarnation of Christ—the divine taking on human flesh in the likeness of sinful humanity. This incarnation holds immense significance in the narrative of redemption, highlighting both the humanity and deity of Christ and His pivotal role as the perfect sacrifice for sin.

Central to the doctrine of the incarnation is the truth that Jesus Christ, the Son of God, willingly entered into the human experience, taking on the frailty and limitations of human flesh. Philippians 2:7-8 beautifully captures this reality: "but emptied himself, by taking the form of a servant, being born in the likeness of men. And being found in human form, he humbled himself by becoming obedient to the point of death, even death on a cross." In His incarnation, Christ humbled Himself, demonstrating His deep love and solidarity with humanity.

The significance of Christ's incarnation lies not only in His humanity but also in His deity. In John 1:14, we read, "And the Word became flesh and dwelt among us, and we have seen his glory, glory as of the only Son from the Father, full of grace and truth." Here, John affirms the divine nature of Christ, emphasizing His eternal preexistence and His role as the Son of God incarnate.

The purpose of Christ's incarnation is twofold: to identify with humanity in its fallen state and to provide the ultimate solution for sin. Hebrews 2:14-15 elucidates this truth: "Since therefore the children share in flesh and blood, he himself likewise partook of the same things, that through death he might destroy the one who has the power of death, that is, the devil, and deliver all those who through fear of death were subject to lifelong slavery." In His incarnation, Christ came to conquer sin and death, offering Himself as the perfect sacrifice for the sins of humanity.

Through His incarnation, Christ not only condemned sin in the flesh but also provided a way for humanity to be reconciled to God. 2 Corinthians 5:21 declares, "For our sake he made him to be sin who knew no sin, so that in him we might become the righteousness of God." In Christ, believers are united with Him in His death and resurrection, experiencing forgiveness, reconciliation, and newness of life.

The incarnation of Christ stands as a testament to the depth of God's love for humanity and the extent of His redemptive plan. Through His incarnation, Christ identified with humanity in its fallen state, providing the perfect sacrifice for sin and offering reconciliation and salvation to all who believe. May we marvel at the mystery of the incarnation and embrace the salvation offered to us through the incarnate Son of God.

The Fulfillment Of The Law In Christ

In Romans 8:3, the apostle Paul unveils the profound truth of Christ's fulfillment of the righteous requirements of the law on behalf of believers. This fulfillment stands as a cornerstone of the Christian faith, highlighting the unique role of Christ as the perfect fulfillment of God's law and the provider of righteousness that the law could not offer.

The Old Testament law, given to Israel through Moses, served as a standard of righteousness and a reflection of God's holiness. However, the law was powerless to save humanity, for no one could perfectly fulfill its righteous requirements (Romans 3:20). The law exposed humanity's sinfulness and inadequacy, leading to condemnation and death (Romans 7:10).

In contrast, Christ came to fulfill the law and accomplish what humanity could not. Matthew 5:17 records Jesus' own words: "Do not think that I have come to abolish the Law or the Prophets; I have not come to abolish them but to fulfill them." In His life, death, and resurrection, Christ perfectly fulfilled the righteous requirements of the law, offering Himself as the ultimate sacrifice for sin and providing the righteousness that the law demanded.

The apostle Paul elaborates on the significance of Christ's fulfillment of the law in Romans 10:4: "For Christ is the end of the law for righteousness to everyone who believes." Here, Paul emphasizes that Christ is the culmination and fulfillment of the law, bringing an end to its condemnation and providing righteousness for all who believe in Him. Through faith in Christ, believers are justified and declared righteous before God, not based on their own merits or works, but on the righteousness of Christ imputed to them (Philippians 3:9).

Furthermore, Galatians 3:13-14 highlights the redemptive work of Christ in fulfilling the law: "Christ redeemed us from the curse of the law by becoming a curse for us—for it is written, 'Cursed is everyone who is hanged on a tree'—so that in Christ Jesus the blessing of Abraham might come to the Gentiles, so that we might receive the promised Spirit through faith." Through His sacrificial death on the cross, Christ redeemed believers from the curse of the law, providing the blessings of salvation and the indwelling presence of the Holy Spirit.

In conclusion, the fulfillment of the law in Christ demonstrates the perfection and sufficiency of His redemptive work. Through His obedience unto death, Christ accomplished what the law could not, providing righteousness and salvation for all who believe. May we rejoice in the fulfillment found in Christ and live in the freedom and righteousness secured for us through His finished work on the cross.

The Condemnation Of Sin In The Flesh

In Romans 8:3, Paul delves into the transformative work of Christ in condemning sin in the flesh—a foundational aspect of the Christian faith that brings freedom from the power and penalty of sin for believers. This truth underscores the redemptive significance of Christ's death and resurrection and its implications for the lives of believers.

Sin, with its devastating consequences, holds humanity in bondage, enslaving individuals to its power and subjecting them to the penalty of death (Romans 6:23). However, through His sacrificial death on the cross and victorious resurrection, Christ dealt a decisive blow to sin, condemning it in the flesh and providing freedom for believers.

The apostle Paul elaborates on the significance of Christ's condemnation of sin in Romans 8:2-3: "For the law of the Spirit of life has set you free in Christ Jesus from the law of sin and death. For God has done what the law, weakened by the flesh, could not do. By sending his own Son in the likeness of sinful flesh and for sin, he condemned sin in the flesh." Here, Paul underscores the inadequacy of the law to overcome sin and highlights the redemptive work of Christ in condemning sin through His incarnation, death, and resurrection.

Through His death on the cross, Christ bore the penalty of sin in our place, taking upon Himself the sins of humanity and satisfying the rightcous demands of God's justice (Isaiah 53:5; 2 Corinthians 5:21). As a result, believers are set free from the power and penalty of sin, experiencing forgiveness, reconciliation, and newness of life in Christ (Colossians 1:13-14).

The resurrection of Christ further validates His victory over sin and death, demonstrating His power to overcome the forces of darkness and to offer eternal life to all who believe in Him (1 Corinthians 15:55-57). Through His resurrection, Christ triumphed over sin, death, and the grave, providing believers with the assurance of victory and the hope of resurrection.

The condemnation of sin in the flesh through Christ's death and resurrection stands as a testament to the power and sufficiency of His redemptive work. Through His sacrificial death and victorious resurrection, Christ provides freedom from the power and penalty of sin for all who believe in Him. May we embrace this truth with gratitude and live in the fullness of the freedom and victory secured for us through Christ's finished work on the cross.

The Role Of Sacrifice In Redemption

At the heart of the Christian faith lies the sacrificial aspect of Christ's work on the cross—an unparalleled demonstration of love and grace that atoned for the sins of humanity, offering forgiveness and reconciliation to God. In Romans 8:3, Paul alludes to this profound truth, inviting believers to explore the redemptive significance of Christ's sacrificial death.

The sacrificial aspect of Christ's work on the cross finds its roots in the rich tapestry of Old Testament imagery and prophecy. Throughout the Old Testament, sacrifices were offered as a means of atoning for sin and reconciling humanity to God (Leviticus 17:11). These sacrifices served as a foreshadowing of the ultimate sacrifice to come—the Lamb of God who would take away the sins of the world (John 1:29).

Christ's sacrificial death on the cross fulfilled the righteous requirements of God's justice, providing the perfect atonement for sin. Hebrews 9:22 affirms this truth: "Indeed, under the law almost everything is purified with blood, and without the shedding of blood there is no forgiveness of sins." Through His shed blood, Christ offered Himself as the perfect sacrifice, bearing the sins of humanity and satisfying the demands of God's justice.

The apostle Paul expounds on the redemptive significance of Christ's sacrifice in Romans 5:8-9: "But God shows his love for us in that while we were still sinners, Christ died for us. Since, therefore, we have now been justified by his blood, much more shall we be saved by him from the wrath of God." Here, Paul emphasizes the sacrificial love of God demonstrated in Christ's death, which justifies believers and saves them from the wrath of God.

Furthermore, Christ's sacrifice on the cross paved the way for forgiveness and reconciliation between God and humanity. Colossians 1:20 proclaims, "and through him to reconcile to himself all things, whether on earth or in heaven, making peace by the blood of his cross." Through His sacrificial death, Christ reconciled believers to God, restoring the broken relationship caused by sin and making peace through His blood.

The role of sacrifice in redemption underscores the centrality of Christ's death on the cross in the plan of salvation. Through His sacrificial death, Christ atoned for the sins of humanity, offering forgiveness, justification, and reconciliation to God. May we never cease to marvel at the depth of God's love demonstrated in Christ's sacrificial sacrifice, and may we embrace the forgiveness and reconciliation offered to us through His finished work on the cross.

The Victory Over Sin And Death

In Romans 8:3, Paul unveils the triumphant victory that believers have through Christ over sin and death—an essential aspect of the Christian faith that underscores the transformative power of His redemptive work in their lives. This victory stands as a cornerstone of the Christian hope, offering believers assurance and confidence in the face of sin and death.

Sin, with its enslaving power and devastating consequences, holds humanity in bondage, leading to spiritual death and separation from God (Romans 6:23). However, through His sacrificial death and victorious resurrection, Christ conquered sin and death, offering believers victory and newness of life.

The victory over sin and death is rooted in Christ's redemptive work on the cross. 1 Corinthians 15:55-57 celebrates this victory: "O death, where is your victory? O death, where is your sting? The sting of death is sin, and the power of sin is the law. But thanks be to God, who gives us the victory through our Lord Jesus Christ." Through His death and resurrection, Christ defeated sin and death, breaking their power and securing victory for believers.

Moreover, the victory over sin and death is not merely a future hope but a present reality for believers. Romans 6:4 declares, "We were buried therefore with him by baptism into death, in order that, just as Christ was raised from the dead by the glory of the Father, we too might walk in newness of life." Through our union with Christ, believers share in His death and resurrection, experiencing newness of life and freedom from the power of sin.

The victory over sin and death also brings assurance of eternal life for believers. John 11:25-26 records Jesus' words: "I am the resurrection and the life. Whoever believes in me, though he die, yet shall he live, and everyone who lives and believes in me shall never die. Do you believe this?" Through faith in Christ, believers have the assurance of resurrection and eternal life, overcoming the fear of death and experiencing the hope of glory.

The victory over sin and death through Christ stands as a testament to the power and sufficiency of His redemptive work. Through His death and resurrection, believers are set free from the power and penalty of sin, experiencing newness of life, assurance of salvation, and the hope of eternal life. May we rejoice in the victory secured for us through Christ's finished work on the cross and live in the fullness of His transformative power in our lives.

The Importance Of Identification With Christ

In Romans 8:3, Paul underscores the importance of believers being united with Christ in His death and resurrection—a profound truth that leads to a newness of life and a right standing with God. This aspect of Christian doctrine highlights the transformative power of Christ's redemptive work and its implications for the lives of believers.

Identification with Christ involves more than mere acknowledgment of His death and resurrection; it entails a spiritual union with Him that brings about profound transformation in the life of the believer. Galatians 2:20 beautifully captures this truth: "I have been crucified with Christ. It is no longer I who live, but Christ who lives in me. And the life I now live in the flesh I live by faith in the Son of God, who loved me and gave himself for me." Through our identification with Christ, believers are united with Him in His death, burial, and resurrection, experiencing spiritual rebirth and renewal.

The importance of identification with Christ lies in its transformative power to bring about a newness of life. Romans 6:4-5 explains this transformation: "We were buried therefore with him by baptism into death, in order that, just as Christ was raised from the dead by the glory of the Father, we too might walk in newness of life. For if we have been united with him in a death like his, we shall certainly be united with him in a resurrection like his." Through our identification with Christ, we experience spiritual resurrection, being raised to new life and empowered to live victoriously over sin.

Furthermore, identification with Christ leads to a right standing with God. 2 Corinthians 5:21 affirms this truth: "For our sake he made him to be sin who knew no sin, so that in him we might become the righteousness of God." Through our union with Christ, we are clothed with His righteousness, standing blameless before God and accepted as His beloved children.

Identification with Christ also fosters intimacy and communion with Him. Philippians 3:10-11 expresses this desire: "that I may know him and the power of his resurrection, and may share his sufferings, becoming like him in his death, that by any means possible I may attain the resurrection from the dead." Through our identification with Christ, we participate in His sufferings and share in the fellowship of His resurrection, deepening our relationship with Him.

The importance of identification with Christ lies in its transformative power to bring about a newness of life, a right standing with God, and intimate communion with Him. Through our union with Christ in His death and resurrection, we experience spiritual rebirth, empowerment, and intimacy with their Savior. May we embrace this truth with gratitude and live in the fullness of our identification with Christ, walking in newness of life and experiencing the abundant blessings of our union with Him.

The Contrast Between Law And Grace

In Romans 8:3, Paul draws a sharp contrast between the law, which brings condemnation, and grace, which brings salvation through faith in Christ. This juxtaposition highlights the superiority of grace in the Christian life and underscores the transformative power of God's unmerited favor.

The law, with its righteous requirements and commands, serves as a reflection of God's holiness and standards of righteousness. However, the law also exposes humanity's sinful nature and inability to meet its demands, leading to condemnation and death (Romans 3:20; Romans 7:7). Galatians 3:10 emphasizes the curse of the law: "For all who rely on works of the law are under a curse; for it is written, 'Cursed be everyone who does not abide by all things written in the Book of the Law, and do them.'"

In contrast, grace represents God's unmerited favor and love extended to humanity through Christ's sacrificial death on the cross. Ephesians 2:8-9 beautifully captures this truth: "For by grace you have been saved through faith. And this is not your own doing; it is the gift of God, not a result of works, so that no one may boast." Through His grace, God offers forgiveness, reconciliation, and salvation to all who believe in Christ, regardless of their merit or performance.

The superiority of grace in the Christian life lies in its transformative power to bring about redemption and restoration. Romans 6:14 declares, "For sin will have no dominion over you, since you are not under law but under grace." Under the law, humanity is enslaved to sin and subject to its power, but under grace, believers experience freedom and victory over sin.

Moreover, grace not only brings salvation but also empowers believers to live lives that are pleasing to God. Titus 2:11-12 affirms this truth: "For the grace of God has appeared, bringing salvation for all people, training us to renounce ungodliness and worldly passions, and to live self-controlled, upright, and godly lives in the present age." Through the enabling power of grace, believers are empowered to manifest the fruits of righteousness in their lives.

The contrast between law and grace underscores the fundamental difference between works-based righteousness and faith-based salvation. Romans 3:21-22 summarizes this contrast: "But now the righteousness of God has been manifested apart from the law, although the Law and the Prophets bear witness to it—the righteousness of God through faith in Jesus Christ for all who believe." Through faith in Christ, believers are justified and declared righteous before God, not based on their own works, but on the righteousness of Christ imputed to us.

The contrast between law and grace highlights the superiority of grace in the Christian life. While the law brings condemnation and exposes humanity's sinful nature, grace brings salvation and empowers believers to live lives that are pleasing to God. May we embrace the richness of God's grace and live in the freedom and victory secured for us through faith in Christ.

Romans 8:5-8:

As we delve into the profound truths of Romans 8:5-8, we confront common misunderstandings surrounding the concept of spiritual living. In a world filled with competing ideologies and philosophies, the notion of life in the Spirit may appear elusive or abstract to many. Yet, in these verses, the apostle Paul offers clarity and insight into the transformative power of the Holy Spirit in the life of the believer.

Far too often, spiritual living is reduced to mere external behaviors or religious rituals, disconnected from the heart and devoid of true intimacy with God. Some may equate it with asceticism or legalism, striving to earn favor with God through their own efforts. Others may view it as a passive experience, expecting spiritual growth to occur without intentional pursuit or engagement.

However, Paul's words challenge these misconceptions and invite us into a deeper understanding of what it means to live in the Spirit. He unveils the reality of a life characterized by the indwelling presence of the Holy Spirit—a life marked by transformation, renewal, and intimacy with God.

In this exposition, we are invited to explore the contrast between life in the Spirit and life in the flesh, understanding the profound implications of each for the believer's spiritual journey. Through careful examination of these verses, we will uncover the inherent conflict between the desires of the flesh and the desires of the Spirit, and the transformative power of the Spirit to overcome sin and bring about spiritual renewal.

As we embark on this journey of exploration, may we set aside preconceived notions and open our hearts and minds to the truth of God's Word. May we be inspired to pursue a deeper relationship with

God, allowing the Holy Spirit to lead us into a life of abundant joy, peace, and freedom. Let us now delve into the exposition of Romans 8:5-8, eager to uncover the riches of spiritual living and its transformative impact on our lives.

Life In The Spirit

In Romans 8:5-8, Paul unveils the transformative power of the Holy Spirit in the life of the believer, leading to spiritual renewal, empowerment, and sanctification. This aspect of Christian doctrine emphasizes the indispensable role of the Holy Spirit in bringing about profound transformation in the hearts and lives of believers.

The life in the Spirit is characterized by a dynamic relationship with the third person of the Trinity—the Holy Spirit—who indwells every believer upon their conversion (Romans 8:9). Through the Holy Spirit, believers experience spiritual renewal and empowerment, enabling them to live in accordance with God's will and to bear fruit for His kingdom.

The transformative power of the Holy Spirit is evident in His role as the agent of regeneration and sanctification. Titus 3:5-6 illustrates this truth: "He saved us, not because of works done by us in righteousness, but according to his own mercy, by the washing of regeneration and renewal of the Holy Spirit, whom he poured out on us richly through Jesus Christ our Savior." Through the work of the Holy Spirit, believers are regenerated and renewed, experiencing spiritual rebirth and transformation from within.

Furthermore, the Holy Spirit empowers believers to live lives that are pleasing to God and to bear fruit that is consistent with their new identity in Christ. Galatians 5:22-23 describes the fruit of the Spirit: "But the fruit of the Spirit is love, joy, peace, patience, kindness, goodness, faithfulness, gentleness, self-control; against such things there is no law." Through the empowering presence of the Holy Spirit, believers exhibit these qualities in increasing measure, reflecting the character of Christ to the world.

The life in the Spirit also brings about a deeper intimacy with God and a greater sensitivity to His leading. Romans 8:14 declares, "For all who are led by the Spirit of God are sons of God." Through the guidance of the Holy Spirit, believers are led into deeper fellowship with God, experiencing His presence, guidance, and empowerment in their daily lives.

Life in the Spirit is characterized by the transformative power of the Holy Spirit in the life of the believer. Through His work of regeneration, renewal, and empowerment, the Holy Spirit brings about spiritual transformation, enabling believers to live in accordance with God's will, to bear fruit for His kingdom, and to experience intimacy with Him. May we embrace the life in the Spirit and yield to the transforming work of the Holy Spirit in our lives, allowing Him to lead us into a deeper relationship with God and to empower us for His service.

The Mind Set On The Spirit

In Romans 8:5-8, Paul emphasizes the importance of having a mindset focused on the things of the Spirit—a mindset that leads to life and peace. This contrast between the mindset focused on the Spirit and the mindset focused on the flesh underscores the profound impact of our thoughts and attitudes on our spiritual well-being.

Having a mindset focused on the Spirit entails aligning our thoughts, desires, and priorities with the will of God and the leading of the Holy Spirit. Philippians 2:5 encourages believers to have the same mindset as Christ Jesus: "Have this mind among yourselves, which is yours in

Christ Jesus." This mindset is characterized by humility, obedience, and a desire to glorify God in all things.

The importance of having a mindset focused on the Spirit is underscored by its transformative effect on our lives. Romans 8:6 declares, "For to set the mind on the flesh is death, but to set the mind on the Spirit is life and peace." A mindset focused on the Spirit leads to spiritual renewal, vitality, and peace, while a mindset focused on the flesh leads to spiritual death and destruction.

The contrast between the mindset focused on the Spirit and the mindset focused on the flesh is further elaborated in Galatians 5:19-23. This passage contrasts the works of the flesh, which include things like idolatry, jealousy, and selfish ambition, with the fruit of the Spirit, which includes love, joy, and peace. By setting our minds on the Spirit, we cultivate a disposition characterized by righteousness, holiness, and obedience to God's Word.

Moreover, having a mindset focused on the Spirit enables believers to discern the will of God and to walk in obedience to His commands. Romans 12:2 exhorts believers, "Do not be conformed to this world, but be transformed by the renewal of your mind, that by testing you may discern what is the will of God, what is good and acceptable and perfect." By renewing our minds according to the truth of God's Word and the leading of the Holy Spirit, we are able to discern and obey God's will for our lives.

Having a mindset focused on the Spirit is essential for the spiritual vitality and well-being of believers. By aligning our thoughts, desires, and priorities with the will of God and the leading of the Holy Spirit, we experience spiritual renewal, vitality, and peace. May we continually seek to set our minds on the things of the Spirit, allowing His truth to shape our thoughts and attitudes, and leading us into a life of abundant joy, peace, and obedience to God's will.

The Hostility Of The Flesh

In Romans 8:5-8, Paul illuminates the inherent conflict between the desires of the flesh and the desires of the Spirit—a conflict that underscores the fallen nature of humanity and the need for believers to crucify self and walk in obedience to the Spirit. This tension between the flesh and the Spirit highlights the spiritual battle that rages within every believer and underscores the importance of yielding to the leading of the Holy Spirit.

The desires of the flesh are rooted in sinful inclinations and worldly passions, leading to spiritual death and separation from God. Galatians 5:17 describes this conflict: "For the desires of the flesh are against the Spirit, and the desires of the Spirit are against the flesh, for these are opposed to each other, to keep you from doing the things you want to do." The flesh seeks to gratify selfish desires and indulge in sinful pleasures, leading to spiritual bondage and destruction.

In contrast, the desires of the Spirit are aligned with the will of God and lead to life and peace. Romans 8:6 affirms, "For to set the mind on the flesh is death, but to set the mind on the Spirit is life and peace." The Holy Spirit empowers believers to walk in obedience to God's commands and to bear fruit that is pleasing to Him (Galatians 5:22-23).

The conflict between the flesh and the Spirit highlights the futility of seeking to please God through human effort or works of the flesh. Romans 8:7-8 explains, "For the mind that is set on the flesh is hostile to God, for it does not submit to God's law; indeed, it cannot. Those who are in the flesh cannot please God." Human effort and self-righteousness are incapable of producing true righteousness or pleasing God. It is only through the empowering work of the Holy Spirit that believers are able to walk in obedience and please God.

The solution to the conflict between the flesh and the Spirit lies in crucifying self and yielding to the leading of the Holy Spirit. Galatians 5:24-25 exhorts believers, "And those who belong to Christ Jesus have crucified the flesh with its passions and desires. If we live by the Spirit, let us also keep in step with the Spirit." By crucifying the flesh and walking in obedience to the Spirit, believers experience spiritual renewal, empowerment, and transformation.

God's Word also declares the reality of believers being made new creations in Christ. 2 Corinthians 5:17 proclaims, "Therefore, if anyone is in Christ, he is a new creation. The old has passed away; behold, the new has come." Through faith in Christ, believers are transformed from within, receiving a new identity and nature empowered by the Holy Spirit.

The conflict between the flesh and the Spirit highlights the fallen nature of humanity and the need for believers to crucify self and walk in obedience to the Spirit. By yielding to the leading of the Holy Spirit, believers experience spiritual renewal, empowerment, and transformation, and are made new creations in Christ. May we continually seek to crucify the flesh, walk in obedience to the Spirit, and live as new creations empowered by God's grace and love.

The Indwelling Spirit

In Romans 8:5-8, Paul illuminates the indwelling presence of the Holy Spirit in the life of the believer—a reality that empowers them to overcome sin, bear fruit, and live in accordance with God's will. This aspect of Christian doctrine highlights the intimate relationship between the believer and the Holy Spirit, and the transformative impact of His presence in their lives.

The Holy Spirit takes up residence within every believer upon their conversion (Romans 8:9). This indwelling presence of the Holy Spirit is not merely symbolic or figurative but represents a profound spiritual reality—a reality that empowers believers to live victoriously over sin and to bear fruit that is pleasing to God.

The indwelling presence of the Holy Spirit empowers believers to overcome sin and temptation. Galatians 5:16 affirms, "But I say, walk by the Spirit, and you will not gratify the desires of the flesh." Through the enabling power of the Holy Spirit, believers are able to resist temptation, overcome sinful inclinations, and walk in obedience to God's commands.

Moreover, the Holy Spirit empowers believers to bear fruit that is consistent with their new identity in Christ. Galatians 5:22-23 describes the fruit of the Spirit: "But the fruit of the Spirit is love, joy, peace, patience, kindness, goodness, faithfulness, gentleness, self-control; against such things there is no law." Through the indwelling presence of the Holy Spirit, as stated earlier, believers manifest these qualities in increasing measure, reflecting the character of Christ to the world.

The indwelling presence of the Holy Spirit also enables believers to live in accordance with God's will and to fulfill the purposes for which they were created. Philippians 2:13 declares, "For it is God who works in you, both to will and to work for his good pleasure." Through the empowering work of the Holy Spirit, believers are equipped and empowered to fulfill God's purposes and to live lives that bring glory and honor to Him.

Furthermore, the indwelling presence of the Holy Spirit fosters intimacy and communion with God, enabling believers to experience His presence, guidance, and empowerment in their daily lives. Romans 8:14 assures believers, "For all who are led by the Spirit of God are sons of God." Through the guidance of the Holy Spirit, believers are led into deeper fellowship with God, experiencing His presence and leading in every aspect of their lives.

The indwelling presence of the Holy Spirit is a reality that empowers believers to overcome sin, bear fruit, and live in accordance with God's will. Through His enabling power, believers are equipped to resist temptation, manifest the fruit of the Spirit, fulfill God's purposes, and experience intimacy with Him. May we continually yield to the leading of the Holy Spirit and live lives that bring glory and honor to God, empowered by His presence and grace.

Temples Of The Holy Spirit

In the Old Testament, the presence of the Holy Spirit was manifested in various ways, often descending upon specific individuals for particular tasks or purposes. However, the indwelling of the Holy Spirit in believers represents a significant shift in the way God relates to His people, particularly after the redemptive work of Christ. This subtopic explores this transition and the significance of believers being temples of the Holy Spirit.

In the Old Testament, the Holy Spirit would come upon individuals for specific purposes, empowering them for service or leadership roles. For example, the Spirit came upon judges like Nathaniel, Gideon, and Samson to lead Israel in battle (Judges 3:10; Judges 6:34; Judges 14:6). The Spirit also empowered prophets like Elijah and Elisha to speak God's word with authority (1 Kings 18:12; 2 Kings 2:9-15). However, the Spirit's presence was not permanent and could depart when His work was completed.

Yet, after the redemptive work of Christ, the Holy Spirit takes up permanent residence in believers. 1 Corinthians 6:19-20 declares, "Or do you not know that your body is a temple of the Holy Spirit within you, whom you have from God? You are not your own, for you were bought with a price. So glorify God in your body." Believers are no longer temples made by human hands but are indwelt by the Holy Spirit, who seals them as children of God and marks them as belonging to Him.

Ephesians 1:13-14 further elucidates this truth: "In him you also, when you heard the word of truth, the gospel of your salvation, and believed in him, were sealed with the promised Holy Spirit, who is the guarantee of our inheritance until we acquire possession of it, to the praise of his glory." The indwelling Holy Spirit serves as a seal and guarantee of believers' future inheritance, assuring them of their status as children of God and their eternal security in Him.

Moreover, the indwelling of the Holy Spirit empowers believers for Christian living and service. Acts 1:8 affirms, "But you will receive power when the Holy Spirit has come upon you, and you will be my witnesses in Jerusalem and in all Judea and Samaria, and to the end of the earth." The Holy Spirit equips believers with spiritual gifts and empowers them to bear witness to Christ and to live lives that glorify God.

The transition from the Holy Spirit coming upon individuals in the Old Testament to indwelling believers as temples of the Holy Spirit represents a profound shift in the way God relates to His people. Believers are no longer temporary vessels of His presence but are permanently indwelt by the Holy Spirit, who seals them as children of God, empowers them for Christian living and service, and assures them of their future inheritance. May we treasure the privilege of being temples of the Holy Spirit and live lives that honor and glorify God in all we do.

> The Holy spirit would come upon Saul, under His influence he would do exploits, but when the Spirit left him, Saul would go nuts and eat grass

Adoption As Sons:

Adoption holds a significant place in both ancient and modern societies, representing a legal and social act by which a person is taken into a family to be raised as a child. In the context of Christianity, the concept of adoption carries profound theological implications, especially for believers who are adopted as sons and daughters of God through faith in Christ. This head delves into the privilege and significance of believers being adopted into God's family, exploring the intimacy, inheritance, and assurance of salvation that accompanies this divine act of grace.

I. Adoption in Ancient Hebrew Culture:

In ancient Hebrew culture, adoption was a legal process by which a child was formally taken into a family, often with the same rights and privileges as a biological child.

In Hebrew culture, adopted children would transition from the status of slaves or wards under a guardian to that of sons, especially when they reached adulthood. This transition brought with it newfound privileges and responsibilities within the family.

II. Biblical Foundation of Adoption:

A. God's Initiative:

The concept of adoption as sons is deeply rooted in Scripture, reflecting God's initiative and love toward humanity. Ephesians 1:5 emphasizes God's role in adoption, stating that He predestined believers for adoption as sons through Jesus Christ according to the purpose of His will.

B. Spiritual Adoption:

Through faith in Christ, believers are adopted into God's family and become heirs of His kingdom. Galatians 4:4-7 underscores this truth, stating that believers are no longer slaves but sons, and if sons, then heirs through God.

C. Abba, Father:

Adoption into God's family brings with it a newfound intimacy and relationship with God as Father. Romans 8:15-16 speaks of believers receiving the Spirit of adoption as sons, enabling them to cry out, "Abba! Father!" This term of endearment reflects the intimate bond between believers and their Heavenly Father.

III. Privileges of Adoption:

Adoption grants believers access to a personal and intimate relationship with God as their Father. This intimacy allows believers to approach God with confidence and boldness, knowing that they are loved and accepted as His children (Romans 8:15; Hebrews 4:16).

As a result, believers are heirs of God's kingdom and recipients of His promises. As adopted sons and daughters, believers are entitled to an eternal inheritance that includes salvation, eternal life, and the riches of God's grace (Romans 8:17; Ephesians 1:11-14).

Adoption also provides believers with the assurance of their salvation and the security of their standing as children of God. The Spirit of adoption bears witness with their spirits that they are children of God, confirming their identity and sealing their inheritance (Romans 8:16-17; Ephesians 1:13-14).

IV. Implications of Adoption:

Adoption transforms believers' identities, moving them from a state of spiritual orphan-hood to that of beloved children of God. This new identity shapes their understanding of self and informs their relationship with God and others.

Adoption carries ethical imperatives for believers to live as children of God, reflecting His character and love to the world. This includes living lives of holiness, love, and service, as befitting members of God's family.

It also motivates believers to share the gospel and extend God's invitation of adoption to others. Believers are called to proclaim the good news of salvation through Christ, inviting others to become part of God's family and experience the blessings of adoption.

Adoption as sons and daughters of God is a central theme in Scripture, highlighting the privilege and significance of believers being brought into God's family through faith in Christ. This divine act of grace grants believers intimacy with God, inheritance in His kingdom, and assurance of salvation. As adopted children of God, believers are called to live lives that reflect their new identity, embodying the love, grace, and character of their Heavenly Father. May we cherish the privilege of adoption and live as faithful heirs of God's kingdom, proclaiming His love and inviting others to become part of His family.

> Imagine being the son and rightful heir to a very powerful leader in the world, say the president of OPEC, or another international body. How would you feel to know you wield his power in your hands? Well, the Holy Spirit testifies with us that we are the sons of the most High God, of all power

Freedom From Fear

As adopted children of God, believers experience a profound freedom from fear—a freedom rooted in the assurance of their redemption, adoption into God's family, and the unbreakable love of their Heavenly Father. This subtopic explores the transformative impact of this freedom from fear on the lives of believers, drawing from relevant scriptures that affirm God's faithfulness and love.

I. Redemption and Adoption:

We are redeemed through the precious blood of Christ, forgiven of our sins, and reconciled to God (Ephesians 1:7; Colossians 1:13-14). This assurance of redemption frees us from the fear of condemnation and separation from God.

Not only that, but also through faith in Christ, believers are adopted into God's family and receive the Spirit of adoption as sons (Romans 8:15; Galatians 4:4-7). This divine act of adoption grants believers the status of children of God, assuring them of their inheritance and relationship with their Heavenly Father.

My dad owns the world!

II. Freedom from Fear:

1 John 4:18 declares, "There is no fear in love, but perfect love casts out fear. For fear has to do with punishment, and whoever fears has not been perfected in love." Believers, knowing that they are loved perfectly by God, are freed from the bondage of fear.

Hebrews 13:5-6 assures believers of God's constant presence and faithfulness, stating, "I will never leave you nor forsake you. So we can confidently say, 'The Lord is my helper; I will not fear; what can man do to me?'" This assurance of God's presence dispels fear and instills confidence in believers.

Our confidence is also amplified by the knowledge that nothing can separate us from the love of God. Romans 8:38-39 affirms the unbreakable love of God for believers, stating, "For I am sure that neither death nor life, nor angels nor rulers, nor things present nor things to come, nor powers, nor height nor depth, nor anything else in all creation, will be able to separate us from the love of God in Christ Jesus our Lord." This assurance of God's unfailing love provides believers with enduring confidence and freedom from fear.

III. Transformative Impact:

Believers, freed from fear, approach God with boldness and confidence in prayer, knowing that they are loved and accepted by their Heavenly Father (Hebrews 4:16).

Moreover, in the face of trials and tribulations, believers draw strength from the assurance of God's presence and love, facing adversity with courage and resilience (Psalm 23:4).

As a result, freed from the fear of rejection or persecution, believers boldly proclaim the gospel and fulfill their mission as ambassadors of Christ, sharing the love and grace of God with others (Acts 4:29-31).

Freedom from fear is a transformative reality for believers, rooted in the assurance of their redemption, adoption into God's family, and the unbreakable love of their Heavenly Father. This freedom empowers believers to live lives characterized by boldness, courage, and confidence, knowing that they are loved perfectly by God and that nothing can separate them from His love. May we embrace this freedom from fear and live as faithful witnesses of God's love and grace, sharing His light with a world in need.

"The Lord is my shepherd, I shall not want...." were David's words. Today I can comfortably say, "The Lord is my dad"

The Spirit Of Adoption

The work of the Holy Spirit in bearing witness to believers of their identity as children of God is a foundational aspect of the Christian faith. Through the Spirit of adoption, believers are prompted to cry out, "Abba, Father," and experience intimacy and communion with God. This subtopic delves into the transformative role of the Holy Spirit in affirming believers' identity and fostering a deeper relationship with their Heavenly Father, drawing from relevant scriptures that underscore the Spirit's work.

I. Witness of the Holy Spirit:

We need not blow our own trumpets; the Holy Spirit is doing this from within. Romans 8:16 assures believers of the Spirit's role in bearing witness to their identity as children of God, stating, "The Spirit himself bears witness with our spirit that we are children of God." This inner witness of the Holy Spirit confirms believers' adoption into God's family and assures them of their status as beloved children.

We share a bond so close that it can't be broken nor corrupted: the bond between a child and its father. Galatians 4:6 highlights the Spirit's prompting in believers' hearts, leading them to cry out, "Abba, Father." This intimate term reflects the close relationship between believers and their Heavenly Father, made possible by the indwelling presence of the Holy Spirit.

II. Intimacy and Communion:

Before the coming of the good news, we were alienated from God. We needed a mediator to take us to Him. But now Ephesians 2:18

emphasizes the Spirit's role in granting believers access to God's presence, stating, "For through him we both have access in one Spirit to the Father." Through the indwelling Spirit, believers experience unhindered access to the throne of grace, fostering intimacy and communion with God.

Not only does he give us unhindered access to God, but he is our teacher, guiding us into ALL truth, not some of it.

John 16:13 speaks of the Holy Spirit's role in guiding believers into all truth, stating, "When the Spirit of truth comes, he will guide you into all the truth." This guidance enables believers to deepen their understanding of God's character and purposes, leading to greater intimacy with Him.

Moreover, he intercedes for us, because we may not even know what to pray for. He searches God's heart, and ours too and matches what we may need in the future with the richness of grace in God.

Romans 8:26-27 underscores the Spirit's role in interceding for believers, stating, "Likewise, the Spirit helps us in our weakness. For we do not know what to pray for as we ought, but the Spirit himself intercedes for us with groanings too deep for words." Through the Spirit's intercession, believers experience a deeper level of communion with God, even in times of weakness or uncertainty. Even when we are not verbally praying, the Spirit communes with God on our behalf.

III. Transformative Impact:

The Spirit's witness affirms believers' identity as children of God, providing them with assurance and confidence in their relationship with their Heavenly Father (Romans 8:16). Knowing that we are the children of God gives us confidence to approach Him as the apple of His eye, and to face the world with heads held high.

This places us in a deeper intimacy with God, for we are assured of His love and good intentions for us. Through the Spirit's work, believers experience a deepening intimacy and communion with God, characterized by love, trust, and dependence (Galatians 4:6).

As a result, filled with the Holy Spirit, believers are empowered to fulfill their mission as ambassadors of Christ, sharing the love and grace of God with others and inviting them into a relationship with their Heavenly Father (Acts 1:8). This is something we are happy and eager to do, the same way kids in the natural world love to brag about their dads.

The Spirit of adoption plays a vital role in the Christian faith, affirming believers' identity as children of God and fostering intimacy and communion with their Heavenly Father. Through the inner witness of the Holy Spirit, believers experience assurance of their identity, prompting them to cry out, "Abba, Father," and deepening their relationship with God. May we yield to the work of the Holy Spirit in our lives, allowing Him to lead us into a deeper understanding of our identity and fostering a closer walk with our Heavenly Father.

The Indwelling Spirit

The significance of the Holy Spirit's indwelling presence in the lives of believers cannot be overstated. This subtopic delves into how the indwelling Spirit empowers believers for Christian living and sanctification, drawing from the rich teachings of Scripture.

I. Empowerment for Christian Living:

The Holy Spirit serves as the source of power for believers, enabling them to live godly and fruitful lives (Acts 1:8). Through the indwelling Spirit, believers receive divine empowerment to overcome sin, resist temptation, and live in obedience to God's commands.

He also guides believers into all truth, illuminating God's Word and leading them in the paths of righteousness (John 16:13). As believers yield to the leading of the Spirit, they experience greater clarity, wisdom, and discernment in their daily lives.

II. Sanctification:

The indwelling Spirit plays a crucial role in the process of sanctification, transforming believers into the image of Christ (2 Corinthians 3:18). Through the work of the Spirit, believers are progressively conformed to the likeness of Christ, growing in holiness and righteousness. This is in no way a product of their own efforts, but the work of the Holy Spirit leading them through scripture and renewing their minds into concurrence with their true identity in Christ.

When conformed to the image of Christ, it's natural for us to bear the fruits of the Holy Spirit. Galatians 5:22-23 lists the fruit of the Spirit, which include love, joy, peace, patience, kindness, goodness, faithfulness, gentleness, and self-control. These virtues are evidence of the Spirit's work in the lives of believers, reflecting the character of Christ and His indwelling presence. However, striving to acquire these qualities does not make you right with God, nor does it qualify you for the Holy Spirit. Finding mangoes on a mango tree is testimony that it is really a good mango tree, but sticking mangoes to a guava tree would not make it a mango tree!

III. Intimacy with God:

The indwelling Spirit fosters intimacy and communion with God, enabling believers to experience His presence and fellowship in a profound way (Romans 8:15). Through the Spirit, believers cry out, "Abba, Father," expressing their deep affection and relationship with their Heavenly Father.

This is why it's easy for us to pray to our father, who is attentively listening while we commune with Him, and He answers back. The Spirit helps believers in their weakness, interceding for them with groanings too deep for words (Romans 8:26). Through prayer and communion with God, believers are strengthened and empowered by the indwelling Spirit, aligning their will with God's purposes.

IV. Transformational Impact:

The indwelling Spirit brings about transformation in the lives of believers, renewing their minds and hearts and empowering them to live as ambassadors of Christ (Romans 12:2; 2 Corinthians 5:20). Through the Spirit's work, believers bear witness to the power and grace of God, reflecting His glory to the world.

Ultimately, empowered by the Spirit, believers are equipped to fulfill their mission as witnesses of Christ, sharing the gospel with boldness and conviction (Acts 1:8). The indwelling Spirit empowers believers to be salt and light in the world, leading others to faith in Christ. Through the outworking of the Holy Spirit, others see God's glory in us, and are enticed to hear the message of salvation.

The indwelling presence of the Holy Spirit is essential for the Christian life, empowering believers for Christian living and sanctification. Through the Spirit's guidance, believers experience transformation, intimacy with God, and empowerment for witness and mission. May we yield to the leading of the Spirit and allow Him to work in and through us, bringing glory to God and advancing His kingdom on earth.

Romans 8:9-11:

As we continue our journey through the treasure trove of Romans 8, we come to verses 9-11, where Paul unveils further revelations about the transformative power of life in the Spirit. In these verses, we are invited to contemplate the profound truth of our identity as children of God and heirs with Christ.

Paul begins by affirming the foundational reality of the indwelling Spirit within believers. He reminds us that if the Spirit of God dwells within us, then we are not merely fleshly beings driven by worldly desires, but we are, in fact, indwelt by the very Spirit of God Himself. This truth serves as a beacon of assurance, illuminating our path and guiding us in our journey of faith.

But Paul does not stop there. He goes on to declare the life-giving power of the Spirit, affirming that the same Spirit who raised Jesus from the dead dwells within us, giving life to our mortal bodies. This is a truth of staggering significance, for it means that the same power that conquered sin and death now resides within us, empowering us to live victoriously in Christ.

As we meditate on these verses, let us marvel at the wonder of our identity in Christ. Let us be filled with gratitude for the incomparable gift of the Holy Spirit, who not only indwells us but also empowers us to live lives that are pleasing to God.

May this exploration of Romans 8:9-11 deepen our understanding of the transformative power of life in the Spirit and ignite within us a passion to walk in step with the Spirit, allowing His life-giving power to flow through us and transform us from glory to glory. And may it inspire us to live each day in the confident assurance that we are indeed children of God, heirs with Christ, and recipients of His abundant grace.

The Indwelling Spirit

The significance of the Holy Spirit's indwelling presence in the lives of believers cannot be overstated. This subtopic delves into how the indwelling Spirit empowers believers for Christian living and sanctification, drawing from the rich teachings of Scripture.

Holy Ghost Inside

I. Empowerment for Christian Living:

The Holy Spirit serves as the source of power for believers, enabling them to live godly and fruitful lives (Acts 1:8). Through the indwelling Spirit, believers receive divine empowerment to overcome sin, resist temptation, and live in obedience to God's commands. Please note that they don't follow in order to be made right with God, but because it's their nature

He doesn't stop there: The Holy Spirit guides believers into all truth, illuminating God's Word and leading them in the paths of righteousness (John 16:13). As believers yield to the leading of the Spirit, they experience greater clarity, wisdom, and discernment in their daily lives.

II. Sanctification:

The indwelling Spirit plays a crucial role in the process of sanctification, transforming believers into the image of Christ (2 Corinthians 3:18). Through the work of the Spirit, believers are progressively conformed to the likeness of Christ, growing in holiness and righteousness.

Although we are eternally righteous before God, the Holy Spirit helps align our way of to the new reality in Christ. In the end we are justified before men, meaning they can too bear us witness that we are indeed God's children, holy and righteous. This is illustrated to men by us bearing the fruits of the Holy Spirit. Galatians 5:22-23 lists the fruit of the Spirit, which include love, joy, peace, patience, kindness, goodness, faithfulness, gentleness, and self-control. These virtues are evidence of the Spirit's work in the lives of believers, reflecting the character of Christ and His indwelling presence.

III. Intimacy with God:

The indwelling Spirit fosters intimacy and communion with God, enabling believers to experience His presence and fellowship in a profound way (Romans 8:15). Through the Spirit, believers cry out, "Abba, Father," expressing their deep affection and relationship with their Heavenly Father.

The Spirit also helps believers in their weakness, interceding for them with groanings too deep for words (Romans 8:26). Through prayer and communion with God, believers are strengthened and empowered by the indwelling Spirit, aligning their will with God's purposes.

IV. Transformational Impact:

The indwelling Spirit brings about transformation in the lives of believers, renewing their minds and hearts and empowering them to live as ambassadors of Christ (Romans 12:2; 2 Corinthians 5:20). Through the Spirit's work, believers bear witness to the power and grace of God, reflecting His glory to the world. Consider how the disciples, now apostles, were cowering in an upper room before the Holy Spirit descended on them, and how things changed drastically when He came into them. Through their changed personalities and courageous declaration of faith, they were able to make an impact, even on the hardest of hearts.

Even today, empowered by the Spirit, believers are equipped to fulfill their mission as witnesses of Christ, sharing the gospel with boldness and conviction (Acts 1:8). The indwelling Spirit empowers believers to be salt and light in the world, leading others to faith in Christ.

The indwelling presence of the Holy Spirit is essential for the Christian life, empowering believers for Christian living and sanctification. Through the Spirit's guidance, believers experience transformation, intimacy with God, and empowerment for witness and mission. May we yield to the leading of the Spirit and allow Him to work in and through us, bringing glory to God and advancing His kingdom on earth.

Spiritual Life And Death

In the realm of spirituality, the concepts of life and death carry profound significance, representing contrasting states of being that have eternal implications. This head delves into the contrast between spiritual life and death, highlighting the transformative power of the Holy Spirit in bringing believers from death to life. Through an exploration of relevant biblical passages and theological insights, we will examine how the indwelling presence of the Holy Spirit empowers believers to experience spiritual rebirth and newness of life.

I. Understanding Spiritual Life and Death:

Spiritual death refers to the state of separation from God and alienation from His presence due to sin (Ephesians 2:1). In this state, individuals are spiritually dead, lacking communion with God and devoid of the abundant life found in Him.

Spiritual life, on the other hand, entails a restored relationship with God and an abiding communion with Him through faith in Jesus Christ (John 10:10). It is characterized by intimacy with God, obedience to His Word, and participation in His kingdom purposes.

II. The Human Condition:

Scripture teaches that all humanity is born into spiritual death as a result of the Fall, inheriting a sinful nature from Adam (Romans 5:12). Apart from Christ, individuals are spiritually dead, enslaved to sin, and under the condemnation of God's judgment (Ephesians 2:3).

In light of humanity's spiritual condition, there is a pressing need for spiritual rebirth—a radical transformation brought about by the regenerating work of the Holy Spirit (John 3:3-6). Without spiritual rebirth, individuals remain dead in their sins and separated from God.

III. The Role of the Holy Spirit:

The Holy Spirit initiates the process of spiritual rebirth, regenerating the hearts of believers and imparting new spiritual life to them (Titus 3:5). This supernatural work of regeneration is essential for individuals to enter into relationship with God and experience salvation.

Beyond regeneration, the Holy Spirit continues to work in the lives of believers, bringing about ongoing transformation and growth in spiritual maturity (2 Corinthians 3:18). Through the sanctifying work of the Spirit, believers are progressively conformed to the image of Christ, reflecting His character and glory.

IV. The Transformative Power of the Holy Spirit:

Throughout this book, I have made numerous references to the transformative power of the Holy Spirit. Under this subtopic, we uncover what it is, and its importance in our lives

The Holy Spirit liberates believers from the power and dominion of sin, enabling them to live victorious lives over sin's grip (Romans 6:14). Through the Spirit's empowerment, believers are no longer enslaved to their old sinful nature but are able to walk in freedom and obedience to God.

He also confirms believers' adoption as sons and daughters of God, sealing them for the day of redemption and assuring them of their inheritance in Christ (Romans 8:15-17). This adoption into God's family signifies a new identity and relationship marked by intimacy and communion with the Heavenly Father.

The same Spirit who raised Jesus from the dead dwells in believers, imparting resurrection power to them and enabling them to experience spiritual vitality and fruitfulness (Romans 8:11). This resurrection power brings believers from spiritual death to life, transforming them into instruments of God's grace and agents of His kingdom.

V. Implications for Christian Living:

Believers are called to embrace the reality of spiritual life in Christ, living in accordance with their new identity as children of God (Ephesians 4:24). This entails walking in holiness, obedience, and dependence on the Holy Spirit for empowerment.

Armed with the transformative power of the Holy Spirit, believers are commissioned to proclaim the gospel message of salvation and invite others into the abundant life found in Christ (Acts 1:8). Through their testimony and witness, believers serve as channels of God's grace, leading others from spiritual death to life.

The journey of spiritual life is marked by continual growth and transformation, as believers are progressively conformed to the likeness of Christ (Philippians 3:13-14). This requires a posture of humility, surrender, and reliance on the Holy Spirit for sanctification and renewal.

The contrast between spiritual life and death underscores the profound implications of the gospel message and the transformative power of the Holy Spirit. Through His regenerating work, believers are brought from spiritual death to life, experiencing a restored relationship with God and participation in His kingdom purposes. As recipients of God's grace and agents of His redemption, believers are called to embrace the reality of spiritual life, proclaim the gospel boldly, and pursue ongoing growth and transformation in Christ. May we yield to the transformative power of the Holy Spirit and walk in the fullness of spiritual life that God has provided for us.

Resurrection Power

The concept of resurrection power is central to the Christian faith, embodying the transformative work of God in raising believers from spiritual death to newness of life. In Romans 8:11, the apostle Paul speaks of the indwelling Spirit as the source of this resurrection power, enabling believers to overcome sin and death. This essay delves into the significance of resurrection power, exploring its implications for believers' spiritual vitality, victory over sin, and ultimate hope of resurrection.

I. Understanding Resurrection Power:

Resurrection power finds its ultimate expression in the resurrection of Jesus Christ from the dead, demonstrating God's victory over sin and death (1 Corinthians 15:20-22). Through His resurrection, Christ ushered in a new era of spiritual life and power for believers.

Resurrection power extends beyond physical resurrection to encompass spiritual renewal and transformation (Ephesians 2:5-6). It involves the regeneration of believers' hearts by the Holy Spirit, bringing them from spiritual death to newness of life in Christ.

II. The Role of the Holy Spirit:

Romans 8:11 declares that the same Spirit who raised Jesus from the dead dwells in believers, imparting resurrection power to them. This power enables believers to experience spiritual vitality, growth, and victory over sin.

The Holy Spirit serves as the agent of spiritual transformation, working within believers to renew their minds, convict them of sin, and empower them to live godly lives (Romans 12:2; John 16:8). Through the Spirit's work, believers are progressively conformed to the image of Christ, reflecting His character and glory.

III. Implications of Resurrection Power:

A. Spiritual Vitality:

Resurrection power infuses believers with spiritual vitality, enabling them to live abundant and fruitful lives in Christ (John 10:10). It empowers believers to overcome spiritual apathy, lethargy, and complacency, stirring them to fervent devotion and service.

B. Victory Over Sin:

Resurrection power equips believers to overcome the power and dominion of sin in their lives (Romans 6:4). Through the indwelling Spirit, believers are empowered to resist temptation, flee from sin, and walk in obedience to God's commands.

C. Hope Of Resurrection:

Resurrection power gives believers hope in the face of physical death, assuring them of their future resurrection and eternal life in Christ (1 Corinthians 15:51-55). Just as Christ was raised from the dead, so too will believers experience resurrection to glory on the last day.

IV. Application of Resurrection Power:

Believers are called to depend on the Holy Spirit for the outworking of resurrection power in their lives (Galatians 5:16). It is through surrender and reliance on the Spirit that believers experience transformation and victory over sin.

Resurrection power empowers believers to pursue holiness and righteousness, reflecting the character of Christ in their thoughts, words, and actions (1 Peter 1:15-16). It motivates believers to live lives that are pleasing to God, glorifying Him in all things.

Ultimately, believers who are filled with resurrection power become powerful witnesses to the reality of Christ's resurrection and the transformative power of the gospel (Acts 1:8). Their lives serve as a testimony to God's grace and the hope of resurrection that is available to all who believe.

Resurrection power is not merely a theological concept but a living reality for believers in Christ. Through the indwelling Spirit, believers are infused with spiritual vitality, empowered to overcome sin, and filled with hope for the future. As recipients of resurrection power, believers are called to walk in dependence on the Holy Spirit, pursue holiness, and bear witness to the transformative power of the gospel. May we embrace the reality of resurrection power in our lives and live as living testimonies to the power and glory of our risen Savior.

Identity In Christ:

The concept of identity is central to the Christian faith, as believers find their true identity in Christ. Through the indwelling presence of the Holy Spirit, believers' identity is affirmed and their lives are transformed, leading to a renewed mindset and a lifestyle that reflects their newfound identity. This essay explores the significance of identity in Christ, examining how the Holy Spirit empowers believers to live out their identity and walk in the fullness of God's purpose.

I. Understanding Identity in Christ:

Believers' identity in Christ is rooted in the foundational truths of the gospel, including their adoption as sons and daughters of God (Galatians 3:26-27). In Christ, believers are made new creations, with their old selves crucified with Him and their lives transformed by His resurrection power (2 Corinthians 5:17).

Believers are united with Christ through faith, sharing in His death, burial, and resurrection (Romans 6:3-5). This union with Christ forms the basis of believers' identity, as they are identified with Him in His death to sin and raised to newness of life in Him.

II. The Role of the Holy Spirit:

The Holy Spirit affirms believers' identity in Christ, testifying to their status as children of God and heirs of His kingdom (Romans 8:16-17). Through the indwelling presence of the Spirit, believers experience a deep sense of belonging and identity as members of God's family.

By and by, The Holy Spirit renews believers' minds, transforming their thinking and aligning it with the truth of God's Word (Romans 12:2). Through the Spirit's work, believers adopt a kingdom mindset, viewing themselves and the world through the lens of God's truth and purposes.

III. Implications of Identity in Christ:

Believers' identity in Christ frees them from the condemnation of sin and empowers them to live victoriously (Romans 8:1). Knowing that they are forgiven and accepted in Christ, believers are liberated from the guilt and shame of their past and enabled to walk in freedom and grace.

Identity in Christ gives believers a sense of purpose and meaning, as they recognize that their lives are part of God's redemptive plan (Ephesians 2:10). Believers understand that they are called to live for God's glory and to participate in His kingdom work on earth.

Believers' identity in Christ fosters intimacy and communion with God, as they experience the indwelling presence of the Holy Spirit (Romans 8:15). Through prayer, worship, and fellowship with other believers, believers grow in their relationship with God and experience His love and grace in deeper ways.

Our identity in Christ frees us from sin's condemnation and empowers us

IV. Application of Identity in Christ:

Believers are called to embrace their identity as sons and daughters of God, living in the fullness of their inheritance in Christ (Galatians 4:6-7). As children of God, believers have access to the Father's love, provision, and guidance, enabling them to live with confidence and assurance.

Believers who know their identity in Christ live holy and righteous lives, reflecting the character of their Heavenly Father (1 Peter 1:15-16). Through the power of the Holy Spirit, believers are empowered to resist sin and pursue holiness, honoring God in all areas of their lives.

Identity in Christ bears fruit in believers' lives, as they manifest the fruits of the Spirit and demonstrate the reality of their faith through their actions (Galatians 5:22-23). By abiding in Christ and walking in obedience to His commands, believers bring glory to God and bear witness to the transformative power of the gospel.

Identity in Christ is a foundational truth of the Christian faith, affirming believers' status as children of God and heirs of His kingdom. Through the indwelling presence of the Holy Spirit, believers' identity is affirmed and their lives are transformed, leading to a renewed mindset and a lifestyle that reflects their newfound identity. May we embrace our identity in Christ and walk in the fullness of God's purpose, empowered by the Holy Spirit to live as sons and daughters of the Most High God.

Assurance Of Salvation:

Assurance of salvation is a vital aspect of the Christian faith, providing believers with confidence in their relationship with God and their eternal destiny. The Holy Spirit plays a central role in providing believers with assurance of their salvation, testifying to their identity as children of God and sealing them for the day of redemption. This subtopic explores how the Holy Spirit grants believers assurance of salvation, affirming their status as children of God and securing their confidence in Christ.

I. Understanding Assurance of Salvation:

Assurance of salvation refers to the confidence that believers have in their salvation and their eternal relationship with God (Romans 8:16). It is the inner conviction that comes from the Holy Spirit, assuring believers of their identity as children of God and their inheritance in Christ.

It is essential for believers' spiritual growth and confidence in their relationship with God. It provides them with peace, joy, and confidence in their standing before God, enabling them to live in freedom and obedience to His Word.

II. The Role of the Holy Spirit:

A. Testimony Of The Spirit:

Romans 8:16 declares that the Holy Spirit bears witness with believers' spirits that they are children of God. Through the inner witness of the Spirit, believers receive assurance of their salvation, confirming their identity as children of God and heirs of His kingdom.

B. Sealing For The Day Of Redemption:

Ephesians 1:13-14 describes how believers are sealed with the Holy Spirit as a guarantee of their inheritance until the day of redemption. The sealing work of the Spirit ensures that believers are secure in their salvation, protected from spiritual harm, and preserved for eternity.

III. How the Holy Spirit Provides Assurance of Salvation:

A. Adoption As Sons:

The Holy Spirit confirms believers' adoption as sons and daughters of God, enabling them to cry out, "Abba, Father" (Romans 8:15). This intimate relationship with God gives believers assurance of their standing as children of God and their inclusion in His family.

B. Inner Witness:

The Holy Spirit bears witness with believers' spirits that they are children of God (Romans 8:16). This inner witness provides believers with a deep sense of assurance, confirming their identity as children of God and their security in Christ.

C. Fruit Of The Spirit:

Galatians 5:22-23 describes the fruit of the Spirit, which include love, joy, peace, patience, kindness, goodness, faithfulness, gentleness, and self-control. The presence of these fruits in believers' lives serves as evidence of the Holy Spirit's work within them, confirming their salvation and their identity as children of God.

IV. The Implications of Assurance of Salvation:

Assurance of salvation brings believers peace and joy, knowing that they are secure in their relationship with God and their eternal destiny (Romans 5:1-2). This inner peace and joy enable believers to face life's challenges with confidence and trust in God's faithfulness.

Believers who have assurance of salvation approach God with confidence in prayer, knowing that He hears and answers their prayers according to His will (1 John 5:14-15). This confidence in prayer strengthens believers' relationship with God and deepens their intimacy with Him.

Assurance of salvation empowers believers to share their faith boldly and confidently with others, knowing that they have a message of hope and redemption to proclaim (Acts 1:8). This boldness in witness leads to the spread of the gospel and the advancement of God's kingdom on earth.

V. Cultivating Assurance of Salvation:

Believers cultivate assurance of salvation by abiding in Christ and walking in obedience to His Word (John 15:4). As believers abide in Christ, they experience His love, grace, and presence in their lives, deepening their assurance of salvation.

Believers renew their minds with the truth of God's Word, filling their hearts and minds with the promises and assurances of Scripture (Romans 12:2). By meditating on God's Word and memorizing key verses, believers strengthen their faith and confidence in God's promises.

They also cultivate assurance of salvation by communing with the Holy Spirit in prayer and fellowship (2 Corinthians 13:14). As believers yield to the leading of the Spirit and cultivate intimacy with Him, they experience His assurance and peace in their hearts.

Assurance of salvation is a precious gift that the Holy Spirit bestows upon believers, confirming their identity as children of God and securing their confidence in Christ. Through the inner witness of the Spirit, believers receive assurance of their salvation, experiencing peace, joy, and confidence in their relationship with God. As believers cultivate assurance of salvation through abiding in Christ, renewing their minds with God's Word, and communing with the Holy Spirit, they grow in their faith and trust in God's promises. May we embrace the assurance of salvation that the Holy Spirit provides and live with confidence in Christ, knowing that we are secure in His love and grace for eternity.

The Spirit's Role In Sanctification:

Sanctification is a process by which believers are set apart for God's purposes and transformed into the likeness of Christ. The Holy Spirit plays a crucial role in sanctification, empowering believers to grow in holiness and conformity to the image of Christ. This essay explores the significance of the Spirit's role in sanctification, highlighting the transformative work He accomplishes in the lives of believers and the importance of yielding to His transformative work

I. Understanding Sanctification:

Sanctification is the process by which believers are progressively conformed to the image of Christ, becoming more like Him in character and conduct (Romans 8:29). It involves the ongoing work of the Holy Spirit in believers' lives, transforming them from glory to glory (2 Corinthians 3:18).

The ultimate purpose of sanctification is to glorify God and reflect His character to the world. Through sanctification, believers become vessels of honor, fit for the Master's use, and equipped to fulfill God's purposes in their lives (2 Timothy 2:21).

II. The Role of the Holy Spirit in Sanctification:

The Holy Spirit renews believers' minds, transforming their thinking and aligning it with the truth of God's Word (Romans 12:2). Through the renewing work of the Spirit, believers adopt a kingdom mindset, viewing themselves and the world through the lens of God's truth and purposes.

The Holy Spirit empowers believers to walk in concurrence to the image of God, enabling them to live holy and righteous lives (Galatians 5:16). Through the empowering work of the Spirit, believers are enabled to overcome sin and walk in obedience to God's Word.

Through his indwelling, The Holy Spirit produces fruit in believers' lives, including love, joy, peace, patience, kindness, goodness, faithfulness, gentleness, and self-control (Galatians 5:22-23). These fruits are evidence of the Spirit's work within believers, reflecting the character of Christ and demonstrating their sanctification.

III. The Process of Sanctification:

Sanctification is a progressive work that occurs over time, as believers yield to the Holy Spirit's transformative work in their lives (Philippians 1:6). It involves a process of growth and maturation, as believers are transformed from glory to glory by the Spirit's power.

While sanctification is ultimately the work of the Holy Spirit, believers are called to cooperate with Him in the process. This involves yielding to the Spirit's leading, obeying His promptings, and actively pursuing holiness in every area of their lives (Romans 6:13).

God has provided means of grace through which believers experience sanctification, including prayer, Scripture meditation, fellowship, worship, and the sacraments. These means of grace serve as channels through which the Holy Spirit works to transform believers' lives and conform them to the image of Christ.

IV. The Importance of Yielding to the Spirit's Work:

Believers must yield to the Holy Spirit's work in their lives, surrendering their wills and submitting to His leading (Galatians 5:25). It is through surrender and submission that believers experience the fullness of the Spirit's power and are transformed into the likeness of Christ.

They must trust in the Holy Spirit's ability to sanctify them and depend on His grace to enable them to live holy and godly lives (Philippians 2:13). It is through trust and dependency that believers experience victory over sin and grow in their relationship with God.

Believers must persevere in the process of sanctification, enduring trials and difficulties with faith and patience (James 1:2-4). It is through perseverance and endurance that believers are refined and purified, becoming vessels of honor fit for the Master's use.

V. The Fruit of Sanctification:

Sanctification results in the transformation of believers' character, as they become more like Christ in attitude, behavior, and conduct (Colossians 3:10). Through the sanctifying work of the Spirit, believers exhibit the virtues of Christ-likeness, including love, humility, and compassion.

The sanctified lives of believers serve as a powerful witness to the reality of Christ's transformative power and the truth of the gospel (Matthew 5:16). By living holy and righteous lives, believers attract others to Christ and glorify God in their midst.

The Holy Spirit plays a central role in sanctification, empowering believers to grow in holiness and conformity to the image of Christ. Through the convicting, renewing, and empowering work of the Spirit, believers are transformed from glory to glory, becoming vessels of honor fit for the Master's use. As believers yield to the Spirit's transformative work and cooperate with Him in the process of sanctification, they experience the fullness of God's grace and become effective witnesses to the world. May we embrace the Spirit's role in sanctification and yield to His transformative work in our lives, becoming more like Christ with each passing day.

Romans 8:12-17:

As we delve deeper into the rich tapestry of Romans 8, we encounter verses 12-17, which paint a vivid portrait of the intimate relationship between believers and their Heavenly Father. In these verses, Paul explores the profound implications of our adoption into God's family and the transformative power of the Spirit in shaping our identity as children of God.

Paul begins by addressing believers as debtors—not in the sense of owing a monetary debt, but rather in the sense of owing a debt of gratitude and allegiance to the One who has redeemed them. He reminds us that we are no longer slaves to sin but have been set free by the Spirit of God. This freedom, however, comes with a responsibility—to live lives that are pleasing to God, empowered by the Spirit who dwells within us.

Yet, Paul doesn't present this responsibility as a burden but rather as a privilege—a privilege of being adopted into God's family as His beloved children. He paints a picture of a loving Father who not only redeems us from bondage but also embraces us as His own, showering us with His love and affection.

Central to Paul's message is the role of the Spirit in affirming our identity as children of God. It is the Spirit who bears witness with our spirit that we are indeed children of God, assuring us of our place in His family and prompting us to cry out, "Abba! Father!" This intimate cry reflects the depth of our relationship with God—a relationship characterized by closeness, trust, and affection.

As we journey through these verses, let us reflect on the profound truth of our adoption into God's family. Let us marvel at the depth of His love for us and the privilege of being called His children. And let us be filled with gratitude for the indwelling Spirit who confirms our identity and empowers us to live as heirs of God and co-heirs with Christ.

May this exploration of Romans 8:12-17 deepen our understanding of the Father's love for us and ignite within us a passion to live lives that are worthy of our calling as children of God. And may it draw us ever closer to the heart of our Heavenly Father, who delights in calling us His own.

Joint Suffering And Glory:

Romans 8:17 reveals a profound truth about the relationship between suffering and glory in the life of believers. This passage highlights the promise of future glory that awaits those who share in Christ's sufferings, emphasizing the eternal perspective that believers are called to embrace. This essay explores the concept of joint suffering and glory, examining its significance for believers and the hope it provides amidst trials and tribulations.

I. Understanding Joint Suffering and Glory:

Romans 8:17 speaks of believers being heirs of God and co-heirs with Christ, sharing in His sufferings and glory. This concept emphasizes the intimate union that believers have with Christ and the solidarity they share in His redemptive work.

The suffering experienced by believers in this present age is contrasted with the future glory that awaits them in the kingdom of God. This promise of future glory serves as a source of hope and encouragement for believers as they endure trials and tribulations in this life.

II. The Relationship Between Suffering and Glory:

Philippians 3:10 speaks of believers sharing in Christ's sufferings, participating in His redemptive work through their own experiences of suffering. As believers identify with Christ in His sufferings, they are conformed to His image and draw closer to Him in fellowship.

1 Peter 4:13 encourages believers to rejoice insofar as they share Christ's sufferings, knowing that they are blessed and favored by God. The fellowship of Christ's sufferings deepens believers' intimacy with Him and strengthens their faith in His promises.

2 Corinthians 4:17 reminds believers that their present sufferings are preparing them for an eternal weight of glory beyond all comparison. The temporary nature of earthly suffering is contrasted with the eternal glory that awaits believers in the presence of God.

III. The Hope of Future Glory:

Romans 8:18 calls believers to adopt an eternal perspective, recognizing that the sufferings of this present age are not worth comparing with the glory that will be revealed to them. Though we may experience trials and tribulations, for a while, they can't compare with the ultimate joy of meeting Christ up in the clouds, enjoying sin-free heaven forever, and judging angels and humans alike. This perspective enables believers to endure trials and tribulations with hope and confidence in God's faithfulness.

Romans 8:30 assures believers that those whom God predestined, called, justified, and glorified will experience the fullness of His salvation. This assurance of salvation provides believers with confidence in their identity as children of God and heirs of His kingdom.

IV. Enduring Trials With Hope:

A. Perseverance in Suffering: James 1:12 encourages believers to persevere under trials, knowing that the testing of their faith produces steadfastness and leads to the crown of life. The promise of future glory motivates believers to endure trials with hope and perseverance.

B. Joy in Suffering: Romans 5:3-5 teaches believers to rejoice in their sufferings, knowing that suffering produces endurance, character, and hope. The joy experienced in suffering is rooted in the assurance of God's love and the promise of future glory.

Joint suffering and glory reveal the intimate union that believers have with Christ and the hope that sustains them amidst trials and tribulations. As heirs of God and co-heirs with Christ, believers share in His sufferings and glory, participating in His redemptive work and anticipating the eternal glory that awaits them in the kingdom of God. May we embrace the promise of future glory and endure trials with hope, knowing that our present sufferings are preparing us for an eternal weight of glory beyond all comparison.

Romans 8:18-25:

As we journey further into the depths of Romans 8, we arrive at verses 18-25, where Paul invites us to contemplate the profound mystery of suffering and hope. In these verses, we are confronted with the reality of present sufferings and the eager anticipation of future glory, as we eagerly await the redemption of our bodies and the culmination of God's redemptive plan.

Paul begins by acknowledging the reality of suffering in the present age—a reality that we all too often experience in our lives. He speaks of the "sufferings of this present time," recognizing the pain and hardship that accompany life in a fallen world. Yet, even in the midst of these sufferings, Paul offers a message of hope—a hope that transcends the trials and tribulations of this world.

Central to Paul's message is the concept of future glory—a glory that far outweighs any suffering we may endure in the present. He speaks of the "glory that is to be revealed to us," painting a picture of a future reality where all creation will be liberated from its bondage to decay and brought into the glorious freedom of the children of God.

But Paul doesn't stop there. He goes on to speak of the eager anticipation with which we await this future glory—a hope that sustains us in the midst of our present sufferings. He describes creation itself as groaning in anticipation of its redemption, longing for the day when it will be restored to its original perfection.

As we delve into these verses, let us be reminded of the tension between present sufferings and future glory—a tension that is central to the Christian experience. Let us take comfort in the hope that we have in Christ, knowing that our present sufferings are but temporary and will one day be eclipsed by the glory that awaits us.

May this exploration of Romans 8:18-25 deepen our understanding of the redemptive work of God and ignite within us a longing for the day when all creation will be restored. And may it inspire us to persevere in faith, knowing that our hope is secure in the promises of our Heavenly Father, who is faithful to fulfill all His purposes.

The Groaning Of Creation:

Introduction:

Romans 8:18-25 delves into the profound concept of creation groaning in anticipation of its redemption. This passage underscores the interconnectedness of humanity and the natural world, highlighting the pervasive impact of sin on the created order. Through exploring the groaning of creation, we gain insight into the universal longing for restoration and the ultimate hope of redemption. This essay explores the significance of creation's groaning, drawing from Scripture to illuminate its interconnectedness with humanity and the longing for renewal.

I. Understanding Creation's Groaning:

A. Scriptural Foundation:

Romans 8:19-22 describes creation's groaning in anticipation of its redemption. This groaning reflects the pervasive impact of sin on the natural world and the universal longing for restoration and renewal.

B. Interconnectedness Of Humanity And Creation:

Genesis 1:26-28 highlights humanity's role as stewards of creation, entrusted with the responsibility to care for and cultivate the earth.

The well-being of humanity is intricately linked to the well-being of the natural world, emphasizing the interconnectedness of all living beings.

II. The Impact of Sin on the Created Order:

A. Genesis 3:17-19 depicts the consequences of humanity's disobedience in the Garden of Eden, including the introduction of thorns and thistles, toil and labor, and eventual death. This passage illustrates the far-reaching effects of sin on the created order, leading to suffering, decay, and disorder.

B. Romans 5:12 further elucidates the universal impact of sin, affirming that through one man, Adam, sin entered the world, and death through sin. As a result of Adam's disobedience, the entire creation was subjected to futility and bondage to decay, groaning in anticipation of liberation and redemption.

III. The Longing for Redemption and Restoration:

A. Romans 8:20-21 describes creation's eager expectation for the revealing of the sons of God, anticipating its liberation from bondage to decay and participation in the glorious freedom of God's children. This longing reflects creation's innate desire for renewal and restoration.

B. Revelation 21:1-5 paints a vivid picture of the new heaven and new earth, where God will dwell with His people, and there will be no more death, mourning, crying, or pain. This vision of the future underscores the hope of redemption and restoration that awaits creation and humanity alike.

IV. The Call to Stewardship and Care:

Psalm 24:1 proclaims, "The earth is the Lord's, and everything in it, the world, and all who live in it." As stewards of God's creation, believers are called to care for and cultivate the earth, recognizing its inherent value and worth.

Matthew 25:40 reminds believers that whatever they do for the least of these, they do unto Christ Himself. This passage emphasizes the interconnectedness of humanity and creation, calling believers to compassionately care for the earth and its inhabitants.

The groaning of creation serves as a poignant reminder of the pervasive impact of sin on the natural world and the universal longing for redemption and restoration. As stewards of God's creation, believers are called to care for and cultivate the earth, recognizing its inherent value and worth. May we heed the call to stewardship and work towards the renewal and restoration of the earth, eagerly anticipating the day when creation will be liberated from bondage and participate in the glorious freedom of God's children.

The Hope Of Redemption:

Romans 8:18-25 offers profound insights into the hope of redemption that sustains believers through trials and tribulations. Paul's perspective on the future glory that awaits believers provides a source of encouragement and strength amidst suffering and uncertainty. This essay explores the hope of redemption, drawing from Paul's perspective and Scripture to illuminate its significance in sustaining believers through trials and tribulations.

I. Understanding the Hope of Redemption:

Romans 8:18-25 emphasizes the future glory that awaits believers, contrasting the present sufferings with the glory that will be revealed to them. This passage underscores the transformative power of hope in sustaining believers through trials and tribulations. We are assured of being transformed into spiritual bodies, devoid of pain and sickness, trials and tribulations, and we know this is from God himself, who cannot lie. We can borrow a leaf from Paul:

Philippians 3:8-11 provides insight into Paul's perspective on suffering and the hope of redemption. Despite facing numerous trials and hardships, Paul remained steadfast in his hope of knowing Christ and experiencing the power of His resurrection.

II. The Role of Hope in Sustaining Believers:

Hebrews 6:19-20 describes hope as an anchor for the soul, firm and secure. This passage highlights the stabilizing effect of hope in the midst of life's storms, providing believers with assurance and confidence in God's promises.

1 Peter 1:3-9 emphasizes the living hope that believers have through the resurrection of Jesus Christ from the dead. This passage encourages believers to rejoice in their salvation, even in the face of trials, knowing that their faith is being refined and tested.

III. The Contrast Between Present Suffering and Future Glory:

2 Corinthians 4:16-18 contrasts the temporary nature of present suffering with the eternal weight of glory that awaits believers. This passage encourages believers to fix their eyes not on what is seen, but on what is unseen, knowing that the trials of this present age are preparing them for an eternal glory beyond comparison.

Romans 8:28 reassures believers that in all things God works for the good of those who love Him, who have been called according to His purpose. This passage emphasizes the sovereignty of God in using even the trials and sufferings of life for His redemptive purposes.

IV. The Assurance of Future Glory:

Revelation 21:1-4 provides a vision of the new heaven and new earth, where God will dwell with His people and wipe away every tear from their eyes. This passage offers believers assurance of the ultimate fulfillment of God's promises and the restoration of all things.

1 Thessalonians 4:13-18 describes the return of Christ and the resurrection of the dead, reassuring believers that those who have fallen asleep in Christ will be raised to eternal life. This passage offers believers hope in the face of death, knowing that they will be reunited with their loved ones in the presence of God.

V. Living in Hope and Expectation:

Romans 15:13 encourages believers to abound in hope by the power of the Holy Spirit. This passage emphasizes the transformative power of hope in filling believers with joy and peace, even in the midst of trials and tribulations.

Colossians 1:27 speaks of Christ in you, the hope of glory. This passage highlights the indwelling presence of Christ in believers, serving as a constant source of hope and assurance in the midst of life's challenges.

The hope of redemption sustains believers through trials and tribulations, providing them with assurance and confidence in God's promises. Paul's perspective on the future glory that awaits believers serves as a source of encouragement and strength, enabling them to persevere in the midst of suffering and uncertainty. May we fix our eyes on the hope of redemption, knowing that our present sufferings are not worth comparing with the glory that will be revealed to us.

> Imagine yourself holding Jesus' hand as you walk through the streets of Glory, angels flanking you on both sides in their pure-white robes

Believers' Assurance And Security In God's Family

Romans 8:18-25 reveals the profound truth of believers being adopted as sons of God, emphasizing the assurance and security that they have as members of God's family and heirs of His kingdom. Despite the present challenges and trials they face, believers find comfort in their identity as children of God, knowing that they are deeply loved and accepted by their Heavenly Father. This essay explores the theme of adoption as sons of God, drawing from Scripture to illuminate the assurance and security that believers have in God's family.

I. Understanding the Theme of Adoption:

In an earlier chapter, I have covered about adoption. It's helpful here, though, to brush up on a few points, so that we understand our definite assurance.

Romans 8:14-17 speaks of believers being led by the Spirit of God and adopted as sons, receiving the Spirit of adoption by whom they cry out, "Abba, Father." This passage emphasizes the intimate relationship that believers have with God as their Heavenly Father.

Galatians 4:4-7 describes believers as heirs of God and co-heirs with Christ, having received the Spirit of adoption as sons. This passage highlights the legal and relational aspects of adoption, emphasizing believers' status as heirs of God's kingdom.

II. The Assurance of Believers' Adoption:

Adoption as sons is not an afterthought on God's part, but part of a big plan for redemption. He had it in mind right from the beginning of time.

Ephesians 1:5-6 emphasizes that believers were predestined for adoption to son-ship through Jesus Christ, in accordance with God's pleasure and will. This passage underscores the sovereignty of God in choosing and adopting believers as His children.

1 John 3:1-2 declares, "See what great love the Father has lavished on us, that we should be called children of God! And that is what we are!" This passage highlights the love and acceptance that believers experience as children of God, finding their identity and security in Him.

III. The Security of Believers' Adoption:

Believers' adoption is an irrevocable premise. The same way you can't reverse the birth of a child, you can't also reverse new birth through the living word of God

Romans 8:38-39 reassures believers that nothing can separate them from the love of God that is in Christ Jesus our Lord. This passage emphasizes the eternal security that believers have as children of God, knowing that His love is unchanging and unwavering.

John 10:28-29 declares, "I give them eternal life, and they shall never perish; no one will snatch them out of my hand." This passage emphasizes the protection and security that believers have in Christ, being held securely in His hand and safeguarded from harm.

IV. The Privileges of Believers' Adoption:

Galatians 3:26-29 describes believers as children of God through faith in Christ Jesus, heirs according to the promise. This passage highlights the privilege and honor of being adopted into God's family, receiving the inheritance promised to His children.

Ephesians 2:19-22 portrays believers as fellow citizens with God's people and members of His household, built on the foundation of the apostles and prophets, with Christ Jesus Himself as the cornerstone. This passage emphasizes the unity and fellowship that believers experience as members of God's family.

V. Living as Sons of God:

When a member of parliament is newly elected, they are taken through a process of orientation, where they are guided on proper house mannerisms, processes I the house and other bitty-gritty as fine dinning. Most of these drills are not put forth as laws but as a limelight into the new life.

To mess up on fine dinning will not disqualify a member from his seat, but may shame him before his peers. Likewise, as the new creation, and sons of the most high God, we may not lose our salvation but are expected to live in a way that reflects God in us.

The same way it's not imaginable to find an MP lying in the middle of the road with a vuvuzela, it's also unimaginable to find a crown prince of heaven with questionable character.

1 Peter 2:9-10 describes believers as a chosen people, a royal priesthood, a holy nation, God's special possession, called out of darkness into His wonderful light. This passage emphasizes the identity and purpose that believers have as sons of God, called to live holy and righteous lives.

Romans 12:1-2 urges believers to offer their bodies as living sacrifices, holy and pleasing to God, as an act of spiritual worship. This passage emphasizes the transformational power of living as sons of God, surrendering to God's will and seeking to honor Him in all aspects of life.

The theme of adoption as sons of God provides believers with assurance and security in God's family, despite the present challenges they face. Through the indwelling presence of the Holy Spirit, believers cry out, "Abba, Father," finding comfort and strength in their identity as children of God. May we embrace our adoption as sons of God, living as heirs of His kingdom and ambassadors of His love and grace to the world.

The Eager Expectation

Romans 8:18-25 unveils the eager expectation of creation for the revealing of the sons of God, highlighting the interconnectedness of humanity and the natural world in their shared longing for restoration and renewal. This profound truth underscores the universal groaning and anticipation for the liberation and redemption of all creation. In this essay, we delve into the eager expectation of creation, exploring its significance and implications, and drawing from Scripture to illuminate its interconnectedness with humanity and the longing for restoration and renewal.

I. The Groaning of Creation:

Romans 8:19-22 describes creation's groaning in anticipation of its redemption, emphasizing the pervasive impact of sin on the natural world and the universal longing for restoration and renewal.

Genesis 1:26-28 highlights humanity's role as stewards of creation, entrusted with the responsibility to care for and cultivate the earth. The well-being of humanity is intricately linked to the well-being of the natural world, emphasizing the interconnectedness of all living beings.

II. The Impact of Sin on the Created Order:

Genesis 3:17-19 depicts the consequences of humanity's disobedience in the Garden of Eden, including the introduction of thorns and thistles, toil and labor, and eventual death. This passage illustrates the far-reaching effects of sin on the created order, leading to suffering, decay, and disorder. B. Romans 5:12 further elucidates the universal impact of sin, affirming that through one man, Adam, sin entered the world, and death through sin. As a result of Adam's disobedience, the entire creation was subjected to futility and bondage to decay, groaning in anticipation of liberation and redemption.

III. The Longing for Restoration and Renewal:

Romans 8:20-21 describes creation's eager expectation for the revealing of the sons of God, anticipating its liberation from bondage to decay and participation in the glorious freedom of God's children. This longing reflects creation's innate desire for renewal and restoration.

Revelation 21:1-5 paints a vivid picture of the new heaven and new earth, where God will dwell with His people, and there will be no more death, mourning, crying, or pain. This vision of the future underscores the hope of redemption and restoration that awaits creation and humanity alike.

IV. The Interconnectedness of Humanity and Creation:

Psalm 24:1 proclaims, "The earth is the Lord's, and everything in it, the world, and all who live in it." As stewards of God's creation, believers are called to care for and cultivate the earth, recognizing its inherent value and worth.

Matthew 25:40 reminds believers that whatever they do for the least of these, they do unto Christ Himself. This passage emphasizes the interconnectedness of humanity and creation, calling believers to compassionately care for the earth and its inhabitants.

V. The Role of Believers in Creation's Redemption:

Romans 8:19-21 portrays creation eagerly awaiting the revealing of the sons of God, indicating that its liberation from bondage to decay is linked to the manifestation of God's redeemed children. This passage underscores the interconnectedness of humanity and creation in God's redemptive plan.

2 Peter 3:13 speaks of a new heaven and a new earth, where righteousness dwells, emphasizing the transformation and renewal of all creation in accordance with God's purposes. This passage highlights believers' role in ushering in God's kingdom and participating in the restoration and renewal of the earth.

VI. Living in Harmony with Creation:

Genesis 2:15 describes God's command to Adam to work and take care of the garden, highlighting humanity's responsibility to steward and nurture the earth. This passage underscores the importance of living in harmony with creation and recognizing its intrinsic value and worth.

Revelation 11:18 speaks of God's judgment on those who destroy the earth, emphasizing the significance of environmental stewardship and the consequences of neglecting our responsibility to care for God's creation.

The eager expectation of creation for the revealing of the sons of God highlights the interconnectedness of humanity and the natural world in their shared longing for restoration and renewal. As stewards of God's creation, believers are called to care for and cultivate the earth, recognizing its inherent value and worth. May we heed the call to environmental stewardship and participate in God's redemptive plan, eagerly anticipating the day when creation will be liberated from bondage and participate in the glorious freedom of God's children.

The Bondage To Decay

Romans 8:18-25 unveils the profound truth of creation's bondage to decay, a consequence of humanity's fall into sin. This passage illuminates the universal impact of sin on the natural world, portraying creation's longing for liberation and restoration. In this exploration, we delve into the depths of creation's bondage to decay, examining its far-reaching implications and the fervent longing for redemption that accompanies it.

I. Understanding Creation's Bondage to Decay:

Romans 8:20-22 describes creation's subjection to bondage and decay, a consequence of humanity's disobedience. This bondage extends beyond the physical realm, permeating the fabric of existence and manifesting in various forms of suffering and deterioration.

Genesis 3:17-19 unveils the repercussions of Adam's sin, ushering in a state of toil and hardship for humanity and the natural world alike.

This passage highlights the interconnectedness of humanity and creation, illustrating the pervasive reach of sin's consequences.

II. The Manifestations of Decay in Creation:

Genesis 6:11-12 depicts a world ravaged by sin, marked by violence and corruption. This passage underscores the degradation of the natural world, mirroring humanity's moral decay and separation from God.

Psalm 107:33-34 portrays the destructive power of sin on the earth, unleashing chaos and upheaval in the form of natural disasters. From floods to famines, creation bears the scars of humanity's rebellion against God.

III. The Longing for Liberation and Restoration:

Romans 8:21 speaks of creation's eager expectation for liberation from bondage to decay, anticipating the revelation of God's redeemed children. This longing reflects creation's innate desire for renewal and restoration, yearning for the day when all things will be made new.

Revelation 21:4 paints a vivid picture of a future free from the shackles of sin and death, where God will wipe away every tear and make all things new. This vision of restoration underscores creation's ultimate destiny, beckoning towards a state of wholeness and perfection.

IV. Humanity's Responsibility in Creation's Restoration:

Genesis 2:15 underscores humanity's role as stewards of the earth, entrusted with the responsibility to care for and cultivate creation. This divine mandate calls believers to champion the cause of environmental stewardship, working towards the restoration of God's good creation.

2 Corinthians 5:17 speaks of believers as new creations in Christ, called to participate in God's redemptive work in the world. This passage highlights the transformative power of the gospel, empowering believers to be agents of renewal and restoration in creation.

Creation's bondage to decay serves as a poignant reminder of the far-reaching consequences of sin on the natural world. Yet, amidst the groaning and suffering, there is hope—a hope rooted in the promise of liberation and restoration. As stewards of God's creation, believers are called to embody this hope, working towards the renewal of all things and eagerly anticipating the day when creation will be liberated from bondage and restored to its intended glory. May we heed the call to care for and cultivate the earth, bearing witness to the transformative power of God's redemptive love in creation's journey towards liberation and restoration.

The Groaning Of The Spirit

Romans 8:26-27 unveils the profound truth of the Holy Spirit's role in believers' lives, especially in times of weakness and groaning. This passage portrays the Spirit as a faithful intercessor, partnering with believers in their journey towards ultimate redemption and glorification. In this exploration, we delve into the depths of the Spirit's groaning, examining His crucial role in empowering and sustaining believers amidst the trials of life.

I. Understanding the Groaning of the Spirit:

Apart from being the royal seal of ownership in us, the Holy Spirit is also our helper. Here are some of the ways he makes our lives easier:

Romans 8:26-27 describes the Spirit's intercession for believers, highlighting His intimate involvement in their lives. This passage underscores the Spirit's deep empathy and understanding of believers' struggles, as He groans alongside them in prayer.

John 14:16-17 portrays the Spirit as the Comforter and Advocate sent by Jesus to be with believers forever. This passage emphasizes the Spirit's role in guiding, comforting, and interceding for believers in times of need.

II. The Spirit's Intercession in Believers' Weakness:

Romans 8:26 speaks of the Spirit's intercession for believers in their weakness, coming to their aid when they do not know what to pray for. This verse highlights the Spirit's omniscience and intimate knowledge of believers' hearts, as He articulates their deepest needs before God.

2 Corinthians 12:9-10 illustrates the transformative power of God's grace in believers' weakness, as His strength is made perfect in their weakness. This passage underscores the Spirit's role in empowering believers to persevere and overcome obstacles through His intercession. We will cover more in the next chapter.

III. Partnering in Believers' Redemption and Glorification:

Romans 8:27 reveals the purpose of the Spirit's intercession—to align believers' prayers with God's will and purposes. This verse emphasizes the Spirit's role in guiding believers towards spiritual maturity and conformity to the image of Christ.

Philippians 1:6 assures believers that God, who began a good work in them, will carry it on to completion until the day of Christ Jesus. This passage echoes the Spirit's commitment to believers' ultimate redemption and glorification, as He works tirelessly to fulfill God's purposes in their lives.

IV. The Spirit's Empowerment in Prayer and Spiritual Warfare:

Ephesians 6:18 exhorts believers to pray in the Spirit on all occasions, with all kinds of prayers and requests. This passage underscores the Spirit's empowerment in believers' prayer lives, enabling them to engage in spiritual warfare and intercession effectively.

Jude 1:20 encourages believers to build themselves up in their most holy faith, praying in the Holy Spirit. This verse highlights the Spirit's vital role in strengthening believers' faith and empowering them to pray according to God's will.

The groaning of the Spirit stands as a testament to His intimate involvement in believers' lives, especially in times of weakness and groaning. As the Comforter and Advocate, the Spirit intercedes on behalf of believers, partnering with them in their journey towards ultimate redemption and glorification. May we lean on the Spirit's guidance and empowerment in our prayer lives, trusting in His faithfulness to lead us closer to God's purposes and plans.

Romans 8:26-27:

As we venture further into the riches of Romans 8, we encounter verses 26-27, where Paul unveils the mysterious workings of the Holy Spirit in the life of the believer. In these verses, we are invited to explore the profound truth of the Spirit's intercession on our behalf and His role in aligning our prayers with the will of God.

Paul begins by acknowledging our human frailty and inadequacy in prayer. He recognizes that there are times when we do not know what to pray for or how to pray as we ought. Yet, even in our weakness, Paul offers a message of hope—a hope grounded in the assurance that the Spirit Himself intercedes for us with groanings too deep for words.

This truth reveals the intimate relationship between the believer and the Spirit—a relationship characterized by communion and partnership in prayer. The Spirit, who knows the mind of God, intercedes for us according to the will of God, ensuring that our prayers are aligned with His purposes and plans.

But Paul's message goes beyond mere reassurance; it also serves as a call to deeper intimacy with the Spirit. He urges us to yield to the Spirit's leading and to allow Him to guide our prayers and petitions. In doing so, we open ourselves up to a deeper experience of communion with God and a greater alignment with His will.

As we delve into these verses, let us be reminded of the privilege we have in prayer—a privilege made possible by the intercession of the Holy Spirit. Let us embrace the Spirit's leading in our prayer lives and allow Him to deepen our communion with God.

May this exploration of Romans 8:26-27 deepen our understanding of the role of the Spirit in prayer and ignite within us a desire to draw closer to God through the power of His Spirit. And may it inspire us to continue our journey of faith, confident in the knowledge that the Spirit intercedes for us according to the will of God, ensuring that our prayers are heard and answered according to His perfect plan.

The Intercession Of The Holy Spirit:

Romans 8:26-27 unveils the profound truth of the Holy Spirit's intercession on behalf of believers, serving as their divine advocate before God. This passage illuminates the significance of intercession in the believer's life, portraying the Holy Spirit as the ultimate intercessor who prays on behalf of believers according to God's will. In this exploration, we delve into the depths of the Holy Spirit's intercession, examining its profound implications for believers and the transformative power it holds in their lives.

I. Understanding Intercession:

Intercession is the act of intervening or mediating on behalf of another, especially in prayer. It involves standing in the gap and pleading for God's mercy, grace, and intervention on behalf of individuals or situations.

It plays a vital role in the believer's life, serving as a powerful tool for spiritual warfare, reconciliation, and divine intervention. It embodies the believer's partnership with God in His redemptive work in the world.

II. The Holy Spirit as the Divine Intercessor:

Romans 8:26-27 describes the Holy Spirit's role as the divine intercessor, who prays for believers in accordance with God's will. This passage underscores the Spirit's intimate involvement in believers' lives, as He intercedes on their behalf with groanings too deep for words.

John 14:26 highlights Jesus' promise of the Holy Spirit as the Helper who will teach and remind believers of all things. This verse emphasizes the Spirit's role as the divine advocate and intercessor, guiding and empowering believers in their journey of faith.

III. The Depth of the Spirit's Intercession:

As humans, we are limited by vocabulary, and our understanding of any language. As such, we may not be effective in prayer, because we only pray for what we can utter and understand. But the Holy Spirit speaks the language of God Himself, and understands more than linguistic syntax.

Romans 8:26 emphasizes the Spirit's intercession with groanings too deep for words, reflecting His profound empathy and understanding of believers' needs and struggles. This form of intercession transcends human language, expressing the depths of the Spirit's compassion and care.

Being part of God Himself, the Holy Spirit knows God's will better than is taught in theology school. This way he doesn't struggle to pray for us in accordance to God's will.

Romans 8:27 reveals the purpose of the Spirit's intercession—to align believers' prayers with God's will and purposes. This verse underscores the Spirit's role in guiding believers towards spiritual maturity and conformity to the image of Christ.

IV. The Impact of the Spirit's Intercession:

The Spirit's intercession empowers believers in their prayer life, enabling them to pray according to God's will and purposes. This partnership with the Holy Spirit strengthens believers' faith and fosters deeper intimacy with God.

The Spirit's intercession provides believers with assurance of God's faithfulness and presence in their lives. His prayers on their behalf serve as a constant reminder of God's unwavering love and commitment to His children.

The intercession of the Holy Spirit stands as a testament to His intimate involvement in believers' lives, serving as their divine advocate and partner in prayer. As believers yield to the Spirit's leading and guidance, they experience the transformative power of His intercession, enabling them to pray according to God's will and experience His faithfulness in their lives. May we embrace the privilege of partnering with the Holy Spirit in prayer, knowing that He intercedes for us with groanings too deep for words, aligning our hearts with God's purposes and leading us into greater intimacy with our Heavenly Father.

Empowering Prayer:

Prayer is the lifeline of the believer, a sacred communion with the divine that transcends earthly limitations. In Romans 8:26-27, we witness the Holy Spirit's pivotal role in empowering believers in their prayer life, enabling them to pray according to God's will and purposes, even in moments of uncertainty. This passage unveils the transformative power of prayer when partnered with the Holy Spirit, illuminating the believer's ability to communicate with God beyond mere words. In this exploration, we delve into the depths of empowering prayer, exploring how the Holy Spirit equips believers to pray in alignment with God's divine purposes.

I. The Holy Spirit: The Divine Enabler of Prayer:

The Holy Spirit serves as the divine guide and enabler in believers' prayer life, leading them into deeper communion with God. His presence empowers believers to pray with clarity, wisdom, and discernment, aligning their prayers with God's perfect will.

The Spirit empowers believers to pray beyond their human limitations, enabling them to access the depths of God's heart and purposes. His supernatural presence infuses believers' prayers with power and efficacy, transforming ordinary communication into divine communion.

II. Praying According to God's Will:

Romans 8:26 underscores the Spirit's role in helping believers pray according to God's will, even when they may not know what to pray for. His intercession aligns believers' prayers with God's divine purposes, ensuring that they are in harmony with His perfect plan.

The Spirit empowers believers to surrender their hearts and desires to God, enabling them to pray with surrendered obedience and trust. His presence prompts believers to yield to God's will, allowing His purposes to be fulfilled through their prayers.

III. Partnering with the Holy Spirit in Prayer:

Prayer becomes a sacred dialogue between the believer and God, facilitated by the Holy Spirit's presence. His intimate communion with believers enables them to pray with boldness, confidence, and faith, knowing that He intercedes on their behalf.

The Spirit intercedes for believers with groanings too deep for words, expressing the depths of their hearts before God. His intercession amplifies believers' prayers, ushering them into deeper intimacy and communion with the Father.

IV. Empowered Living through Prayer:

Empowering prayer transforms believers' hearts and lives, aligning them with God's purposes and desires. The Spirit's presence empowers believers to live a life of prayerful obedience and surrender, bearing witness to His transformative work in their lives.

Empowered prayer equips believers to bear witness to God's faithfulness and power in their lives and the lives of others. The Spirit's presence enables believers to pray with expectancy and faith, ushering in divine breakthroughs and manifestations of God's glory.

Empowering prayer is not merely a religious ritual but a divine encounter with the Living God, facilitated by the Holy Spirit's presence and power. As believers partner with the Spirit in prayer, they experience the transformative power of divine communion, enabling them to pray according to God's will and purposes. May we embrace the privilege of empowering prayer, knowing that the Holy Spirit empowers us to communicate with God beyond mere words, ushering us into deeper intimacy and communion with our Heavenly Father.

Spiritual Warfare And Intercession:

In the spiritual battlefield of life, believers are not left defenseless. Romans 8:26-27 unveils the Holy Spirit's vital role in equipping believers for spiritual warfare through intercession, empowering them to overcome challenges and opposition in the spiritual realm. This passage illuminates the transformative power of intercessory prayer in believers' lives, enabling them to stand firm against the schemes of the enemy. In this exploration, we delve into the depths of spiritual warfare and intercession, discovering how the Holy Spirit empowers believers to walk in victory and authority.

I. Understanding Spiritual Warfare:

Spiritual warfare is soften mistaken for a task that Believers have to actively take part in every second of their lives. The truth is that the only war the believer has to engage in actively is against conceptions and thought.

The war against the devil has been worn, the victory shown in the finished work of the cross. Likewise, the war is not against religions of the world, or kings or individuals.

Ephesians 6:12 reminds believers that their struggle is not against flesh and blood but against spiritual forces of evil in the heavenly realms. This passage underscores the reality of spiritual warfare and the need for believers to be equipped for battle.

The only way to be equipped in this battle is by knowing what the word of God says about the new creation, believing it and making it your reality

1 John 4:4 assures believers that greater is He who is in them than he who is in the world. This verse emphasizes believers' authority and victory in Christ, empowering them to overcome the enemy's schemes through the power of the Holy Spirit.

II. The Role of Intercession in Spiritual Warfare:

Romans 8:26-27 reveals the Holy Spirit's intercession for believers in their weakness, empowering them to pray according to God's will even in the midst of spiritual warfarc. This passage underscores the Spirit's role in strengthening believers and thwarting the enemy's plans.

James 5:16 encourages believers to pray for one another, acknowledging the powerful impact of intercessory prayer in spiritual warfare. This verse highlights the importance of standing in the gap for fellow believers, interceding for their protection and deliverance.

III. Empowered by the Holy Spirit:

Ephesians 6:10-18 describes the spiritual armor that believers are called to put on, equipping them for spiritual warfare. This passage emphasizes the importance of relying on the Holy Spirit's empowerment to stand firm against the enemy's attacks.

His attacks are not against your home, finances or even relationships, but have your faith as the end-game. It's important to be firmly rooted in the word of God, strong in your faith, so that it will never be shaken under whichever circumstances.

2 Corinthians 10:4-5 speaks of the weapons of our warfare, which are mighty through God for pulling down strongholds and casting down arguments. This verse highlights believers' authority and power in Christ, enabled by the Holy Spirit's empowerment.

IV. Walking in Victory and Authority:

1 Peter 5:8-9 exhorts believers to be sober-minded and vigilant, resisting the devil who seeks to devour them. This passage underscores believers' ability to overcome the enemy's attacks through the power of the Holy Spirit.

Ephesians 6:13 encourages believers to take up the whole armor of God and to stand firm in the face of adversity. This verse emphasizes the importance of relying on the Holy Spirit's empowerment to withstand the enemy's assaults and emerge victorious.

In the midst of spiritual warfare, believers are not left to fend for themselves. Through the empowering work of the Holy Spirit, believers are equipped to stand firm against the enemy's schemes and walk in victory and authority. May we embrace the privilege of intercessory prayer, knowing that the Holy Spirit empowers us to overcome challenges and opposition in the spiritual realm, enabling us to walk in victory and authority as children of God.

Aligning With God's Will:

In the journey of faith, aligning with God's will is paramount for believers seeking spiritual maturity and conformity to the image of Christ. Romans 8:26-27 reveals the Holy Spirit's essential role in helping believers align their prayers with God's will, guiding them towards greater spiritual maturity and transformation. This passage illuminates the transformative power of prayer when partnered with the Holy Spirit, leading believers into deeper intimacy with God and conformity to His purposes. In this exploration, we delve into the depths of aligning with God's will, discovering how the Holy Spirit empowers believers to pray in accordance with His divine plan.

I. The Holy Spirit's Guidance in Prayer:

Romans 8:26-27 unveils the Holy Spirit's intercession for believers, helping them align their prayers with God's will even in moments of weakness and uncertainty. This passage emphasizes the Spirit's role in guiding believers towards greater alignment with God's purposes through prayer.

John 16:13 assures believers that the Holy Spirit will guide them into all truth, revealing God's will and purposes for their lives. This verse underscores the Spirit's role as the divine guide, leading believers towards alignment with God's will through His transformative work.

III. Surrendered Hearts and Obedient Living:

Proverbs 3:5-6 encourages believers to trust in the Lord with all their hearts and lean not on their own understanding, but to acknowledge Him in all their ways, and He will direct their paths. This passage emphasizes the importance of surrendering to God's will and seeking His guidance in all areas of life.

1 John 5:14-15 assures believers that if they ask anything according to God's will, He hears them, and if they know that He hears them, they have the petitions that they have asked of Him. This passage highlights the importance of obedient living and aligning one's prayers with God's will.

IV. Conformity to Christ and Spiritual Maturity:

Galatians 5:22-23 describes the fruit of the Spirit, which includes love, joy, peace, patience, kindness, goodness, faithfulness, gentleness, and self-control. This passage underscores believers' transformation into Christ-likeness through alignment with God's will and the work of the Holy Spirit.

2 Corinthians 3:18 reveals believers' transformation into the image of Christ, from glory to glory, by the Spirit of the Lord. This verse emphasizes the ongoing journey of spiritual maturity and growth towards alignment with God's will, empowered by the Holy Spirit.

Aligning with God's will is the heartbeat of the believer's journey towards spiritual maturity and conformity to the image of Christ. Through the empowering work of the Holy Spirit, believers are guided into deeper intimacy with God and alignment with His purposes through prayer. May we embrace the privilege of partnering with the Holy Spirit in prayer, allowing Him to align our hearts and prayers with God's will, leading us towards greater spiritual maturity and transformation.

> We all, with unveiled faces, are looking as in a mirror at the glory of the Lord and are being transformed into the same image from glory to glory; this is from the Lord who is the Spirit.

The Comfort Of The Spirit:

In the midst of life's trials and tribulations, believers find solace in the comforting presence of the Holy Spirit. Romans 8:26-27 unveils the Holy Spirit's role as the divine Comforter, interceding for believers with groanings too deep for words, particularly in times of weakness and uncertainty. This passage underscores the transformative power of the Spirit's intercession, providing believers with strength, reassurance, and hope amidst life's challenges. In this exploration, we delve into the depths of the comfort of the Spirit, discovering how His intercession brings solace and peace to believers' lives.

I. The Promise of Comfort:

Sometimes in our lives we feel like the weight of the world is our shoulders. The good news for us who believe is that we have the Holy Spirit, who is our comforter.

John 14:16 assures believers that Jesus will send another Comforter, the Holy Spirit, who will abide with them forever. This verse highlights the Spirit's role as the divine Comforter, providing solace and reassurance to believers in times of need.

2 Corinthians 1:3-4 describes God as the Father of mercies and the God of all comfort, who comforts believers in all their afflictions. This passage emphasizes God's compassionate nature and His desire to comfort His children through the presence of the Holy Spirit.

II. Intercession in Weakness:

When you are emotional beyond words, when you can't even formulate a few words to say to God, there is the helper who prays for you, in a style impossible to humans.

Romans 8:26-27 reveals the Holy Spirit's intercession for believers with groanings too deep for words, particularly in times of weakness and uncertainty. This passage underscores the Spirit's empathetic intercession on behalf of believers, expressing the depths of their hearts before God.

2 Corinthians 12:9-10 reminds believers that God's power is made perfect in their weakness, enabling them to endure trials and tribulations through the empowering presence of the Holy Spirit. This passage highlights the Spirit's ability to strengthen believers in their times of weakness. Even when you are too weak to pray, the Holy Spirit is at work, praying for you.

III. Reassurance in Uncertainty:

Philippians 4:6-7 encourages believers to be anxious for nothing but to present their requests to God with thanksgiving, and the peace of God, which surpasses all understanding, will guard their hearts and minds in Christ Jesus. This verse underscores the Spirit's ability to bring peace and reassurance to believers amidst uncertainty and anxiety.

Proverbs 3:5-6 exhorts believers to trust in the Lord with all their hearts and lean not on their own understanding, acknowledging Him in all their ways, and He will direct their paths. This passage emphasizes the importance of trusting in God's providence and the comforting presence of the Holy Spirit in guiding believers through life's uncertainties.

IV. Hope in the Midst of Trials:

Faith, the father of hope, is what sustains a believer in the strongest storms. We are assured not only of a better tomorrow, but also of a glorious day.

Romans 15:13 declares that may the God of hope fill believers with all joy and peace in believing, so that by the power of the Holy Spirit they may abound in hope. This verse emphasizes the Spirit's role in sustaining believers' hope and confidence in God's promises, even in the midst of trials and tribulations.

Hebrews 6:19 describes hope as the anchor of the soul, firm and secure, which enters the inner sanctuary behind the curtain. This passage highlights the Spirit's comforting presence as the anchor of believers' souls, providing stability and assurance amidst life's storms.

The comfort of the Spirit is a beacon of hope and solace for believers navigating life's trials and uncertainties. Through His empathetic intercession and comforting presence, the Holy Spirit strengthens, reassures, and sustains believers, enabling them to find peace and hope amidst life's challenges. May we embrace the comforting presence of the Holy Spirit, finding solace and reassurance in His intercession, and trusting in His providence to guide us through life's uncertainties.

Cooperating With The Holy Spirit In Prayer

Prayer is not merely a religious ritual but a profound expression of believers' relationship with God. Romans 8:26-27 reveals the Holy Spirit's vital role in believers' prayer lives, interceding for them with groanings too deep for words. This passage underscores the transformative power of prayer when partnered with the Holy Spirit, leading believers into deeper intimacy with God and alignment with His will. In this exploration, we delve into practical insights on how believers can cooperate with the Holy Spirit in prayer, fostering a deeper relationship with God and experiencing His transformative power in their lives.

I. Cultivating a Spirit-Led Prayer Life:

James 4:8 encourages believers to draw near to God, and He will draw near to them, cleansing their hands and purifying their hearts. This verse highlights the importance of surrendering to God's will and inviting the Holy Spirit to lead in prayer.

1 Kings 19:12 depicts Elijah hearing the Lord's voice in a gentle whisper amidst the noise and chaos. This passage underscores the importance of cultivating a spirit of listening and silence in prayer, allowing the Holy Spirit to speak and lead.

II. Partnering with the Holy Spirit:

Matthew 18:19-20 emphasizes the power of agreement in prayer, assuring believers that where two or three gather in Jesus' name, He is in their midst. This verse highlights the importance of partnering with fellow believers and the Holy Spirit in prayer.

Isaiah 30:21 assures believers that whether they turn to the right or to the left, their ears will hear a voice behind them, saying, "This is the way; walk in it." This passage underscores the importance of yielding to the Holy Spirit's promptings and guidance in prayer.

III. Praying According to God's Will:

1 John 5:14-15 assures believers that if they ask anything according to God's will, He hears them, and if they know that He hears them, they have the petitions that they have asked of Him. This passage emphasizes the importance of aligning prayers with God's Word and purposes.

Matthew 6:33 exhorts believers to seek first the kingdom of God and His righteousness, trusting that all these things will be added unto them. This verse highlights the importance of prioritizing God's kingdom and aligning prayers with His will.

IV. Persisting in Prayer:

Luke 18:1 encourages believers to always pray and not give up, highlighting the importance of persistence and faithfulness in prayer. This verse underscores the transformative power of persistent prayer when coupled with the Holy Spirit's empowerment.

Psalm 5:3 declares that in the morning, believers will hear God's voice and lay their requests before Him, eagerly waiting in expectation. This passage emphasizes the importance of waiting upon the Lord in prayer, trusting in His timing and provision.

Prayer is a divine invitation to commune with God and partner with Him in His redemptive purposes. By cooperating with the Holy Spirit in prayer, believers can foster a deeper relationship with God and experience His transformative power in their lives. May we embrace the practical insights provided by Scripture, yielding to the Holy Spirit's guidance and intercession, and allowing prayer to become a life-giving expression of our relationship with God.

Romans 8:28-30:

As we continue our exploration of Romans 8, we come to verses 28-30, where Paul unveils the majestic workings of God's sovereign plan for His people. In these verses, we are invited to marvel at the intricacy and beauty of God's providence, as He works all things together for the good of those who love Him and are called according to His purpose.

Paul begins by making a bold declaration—a declaration that has brought comfort and assurance to countless believers throughout the ages: "And we know that for those who love God all things work together for good, for those who are called according to his purpose."

In these words, Paul offers a message of hope in the midst of life's trials and tribulations. He assures us that even in the face of adversity and suffering, God is at work, weaving together the threads of our lives into a tapestry of His divine purpose.

But Paul doesn't stop there. He goes on to unveil the grand sweep of God's redemptive plan—a plan that was set in motion before the foundation of the world. He speaks of God's foreknowledge, predestination, calling, justification, and glorification, outlining the various stages of our salvation from beginning to end.

As we delve into these verses, let us be reminded of the sovereignty of God and His unfailing faithfulness to His people. Let us take comfort in the knowledge that no matter what circumstances we may face, God is always at work for our good and His glory.

May this exploration of Romans 8:28-30 deepen our understanding of God's providential care and ignite within us a desire to trust Him more fully with our lives. And may it inspire us to embrace our calling as children of God, confident in the knowledge that He who began a good work in us will bring it to completion at the day of Jesus Christ.

God's Sovereign Control And Purposeful Work

At the heart of the Christian faith lies the profound truth of divine providence, the belief that God exercises sovereign control over all things and works them together for the good of those who love Him. Romans 8:28 stands as a beacon of hope for believers, affirming God's unwavering commitment to His people and His purposeful orchestration of events in their lives. In this exploration of divine providence, we journey through the narrative continuity of Scripture, witnessing God's sovereign hand at work and finding assurance in His faithful provision.

I. God's Sovereign Rule:

Genesis 1:1 declares, "In the beginning, God created the heavens and the earth," establishing God's sovereignty over all creation. Throughout the narrative of Scripture, we see God's orderly governance over the universe, sustaining and directing all things according to His will.

Hebrews 1:3 describes Jesus as the radiance of God's glory and the exact representation of His being, sustaining all things by His powerful word. This verse highlights God's ongoing providential care and involvement in every aspect of His creation.

II. Purposeful Work for Good:

Romans 8:28: "And we know that in all things God works for the good of those who love Him, who have been called according to His purpose." This pivotal verse encapsulates the essence of divine providence, assuring believers of God's commitment to work all things together for their ultimate good.

In Genesis 50:20, Joseph reflects on his tumultuous journey from slavery to rulership in Egypt, recognizing God's providential hand at work in his life. Despite facing adversity and betrayal, Joseph acknowledges that what his brothers intended for evil, God used for good, saving many lives in the process.

III. Trusting in God's Providence:

Proverbs 3:5-6: "Trust in the Lord with all your heart and lean not on your own understanding; in all your ways submit to Him, and He will make your paths straight." This timeless wisdom encourages believers to entrust their lives to God's providential care, acknowledging His sovereignty and wisdom.

In Matthew 6:25-34, Jesus teaches His disciples not to worry about their basic needs but to seek first the kingdom of God and His righteousness. He assures them that their heavenly Father knows their needs and will provide for them, highlighting the loving care of divine providence.

IV. Ultimate Fulfillment of God's Purposes:

Revelation 21:3-5: In the final chapters of Revelation, John envisions a new heaven and a new earth, where God dwells with His people, wiping away every tear and making all things new. This glorious future underscores the ultimate fulfillment of God's purposes and the consummation of His providential plan.

Divine providence is not merely a theological concept but a lived reality for believers, reassuring them of God's sovereign control and purposeful work in their lives. As we journey through the narrative continuity of Scripture, we witness God's unwavering commitment to His people, orchestrating events for their ultimate good and His glory. May we find solace and assurance in the truth of divine providence, trusting in God's sovereign rule and faithful provision in every season of life.

Predestination And Calling:

The theological concepts of predestination and calling delve into the intricacies of God's sovereign plan for salvation, revealing His foreknowledge and sovereign will in choosing believers for redemption. Romans 8:28-30 provides a profound insight into these concepts, assuring believers of their divine calling and the assurance of their salvation. In this exploration, we delve into the biblical foundation of predestination and calling, seeking to understand God's sovereign work in the lives of His chosen people.

I. The Concept of Predestination:

Ephesians 1:4-5: "For He chose us in Him before the creation of the world to be holy and blameless in His sight. In love, He predestined us for adoption to son-ship through Jesus Christ, in accordance with His pleasure and will." This passage underscores God's sovereign choice of believers for salvation before the foundation of the world, highlighting His eternal purpose and pleasure in redemption.

Romans 9:15-16: "For He says to Moses, 'I will have mercy on whom I have mercy, and I will have compassion on whom I have compassion.' It does not, therefore, depend on human desire or effort, but on God's mercy." This verse emphasizes that salvation is not based on human merit or effort but on God's sovereign choice and mercy, illustrating the concept of predestination.

II. God's Sovereign Calling:

2 Timothy 1:9: "He has saved us and called us to a holy life—not because of anything we have done but because of His own purpose and grace. This grace was given us in Christ Jesus before the beginning of time." This verse emphasizes God's sovereign calling of believers to salvation and sanctification, highlighting His eternal purpose and grace.

1 Peter 2:9: "But you are a chosen people, a royal priesthood, a holy nation, God's special possession, that you may declare the praises of Him who called you out of darkness into His wonderful light." This passage underscores believers' identity as God's chosen people, called out of darkness into His marvelous light for the purpose of declaring His praises.

III. Understanding God's Foreknowledge:

Romans 8:29: "For those God foreknew, He also predestined to be conformed to the image of His Son, that He might be the firstborn among many brothers and sisters." This verse highlights the intimate relationship between God's foreknowledge and predestination, illustrating His sovereign plan to conform believers to the likeness of Christ.

Acts 13:48: "When the Gentiles heard this, they were glad and honored the word of the Lord; and all who were appointed for eternal life believed." This verse portrays believers' response to the gospel as a reflection of God's sovereign appointment for eternal life, illustrating the concept of divine calling and election.

IV. Assurance of Salvation:

Romans 8:30: "And those He predestined, He also called; those He called, He also justified; those He justified, He also glorified." This verse provides believers with the assurance of their salvation, highlighting the unbroken chain of God's sovereign work from predestination to glorification.

John 10:27-29: "My sheep listen to my voice; I know them, and they follow me. I give them eternal life, and they shall never perish; no one will snatch them out of my hand. My Father, who has given them to me, is greater than all; no one can snatch them out of my Father's hand." This passage assures believers of the security of their salvation in the hands of the sovereign God who predestined, called, justified, and glorified them.

The theological concepts of predestination and calling provide believers with a profound understanding of God's sovereign plan for salvation. As we delve into the biblical foundation of these concepts, we find assurance in God's eternal purpose and grace, trusting in His sovereign will and foreknowledge. May we embrace the truth of predestination and calling, finding comfort in the assurance of our salvation and the unbreakable chain of God's sovereign work in our lives.

Conformity To Christ:

God's ultimate purpose for believers is to be conformed to the image of His Son, Jesus Christ. This profound truth underscores the transformative journey of sanctification, where every aspect of believers' lives is orchestrated by God to achieve this divine purpose. Romans 8:28-30 provides a glimpse into this transformative process, assuring believers that God works all things together for their ultimate good, conforming them to the likeness of Christ. In this exploration, we delve into the biblical foundation of conformity to Christ, finding assurance in God's sovereign plan and faithful work in the lives of His people.

I. The Image of Christ:

Colossians 1:15: "The Son is the image of the invisible God, the firstborn over all creation." This verse affirms Jesus Christ as the perfect representation of God's nature and character, serving as the ultimate standard of conformity for believers.

2 Corinthians 3:18: "And we all, who with unveiled faces contemplate the Lord's glory, are being transformed into his image with ever-increasing glory, which comes from the Lord, who is the Spirit." This passage highlights believers' ongoing transformation into the likeness of Christ, empowered by the Holy Spirit's work in their lives.

II. God's Sovereign Work of Sanctification:

Philippians 1:6: "Being confident of this, that he who began a good work in you will carry it on to completion until the day of Christ Jesus." This verse assures believers of God's faithful work of sanctification in their lives, ensuring that He will bring it to completion.

1 Thessalonians 5:23-24: "May God himself, the God of peace, sanctify you through and through. May your whole spirit, soul and body be kept blameless at the coming of our Lord Jesus Christ. The one who calls you is faithful, and he will do it." This passage emphasizes God's faithfulness in sanctifying believers entirely, conforming them to the image of Christ.

III. The Transformative Power of Trials:

James 1:2-4: "Consider it pure joy, my brothers and sisters, whenever you face trials of many kinds, because you know that the testing of your faith produces perseverance. Let perseverance finish its work so that you may be mature and complete, not lacking anything." This passage illustrates how trials and tribulations contribute to believers' growth and conformity to Christ's likeness.

Romans 5:3-5: "Not only so, but we also glory in our sufferings, because we know that suffering produces perseverance; perseverance, character; and character, hope. And hope does not put us to shame, because God's love has been poured out into our hearts through the Holy Spirit, who has been given to us." This verse highlights the transformative power of suffering in believers' lives, shaping their character and fostering hope as they are conformed to the image of Christ.

IV. Living as Christ's Representatives:

2 Corinthians 5:20: "We are therefore Christ's ambassadors, as though God were making his appeal through us. We implore you on Christ's behalf: Be reconciled to God." This verse calls believers to live as Christ's representatives in the world, embodying His love, grace, and truth as they are conformed to His image.

Ephesians 5:1-2: "Follow God's example, therefore, as dearly loved children and walk in the way of love, just as Christ loved us and gave himself up for us as a fragrant offering and sacrifice to God." This passage exhorts believers to imitate God and walk in love, following the example of Christ as they are conformed to His image.

Conformity to Christ is the ultimate purpose of believers' lives, where every aspect of their existence is orchestrated by God to achieve this divine goal. As we journey through the transformative process of sanctification, may we find assurance in God's faithful work and trust in His sovereign plan to conform us to the likeness of His Son, Jesus Christ. May we live as Christ's representatives in the world, embodying His love, grace, and truth, and bringing glory to His name.

Justification And Glorification:

The believer's salvation journey encompasses a transformative sequence of events orchestrated by God, from justification to glorification. This journey begins with the act of justification, where believers are declared righteous through faith in Christ, and culminates in glorification, where they are transformed into the likeness of Christ and fully conformed to His image. Romans 8:28-30 illuminates this journey, assuring believers of God's faithful work in redeeming and transforming His people. In this exploration, we delve into the biblical foundation of justification and glorification, finding assurance in God's sovereign plan and unwavering promise of redemption.

I. The Act of Justification:

Romans 3:23-24: "For all have sinned and fall short of the glory of God, and all are justified freely by his grace through the redemption that came by Christ Jesus." This passage underscores the universal need for justification and the gracious provision of God's redemption through Christ's sacrifice.

Romans 5:1-2: "Therefore, since we have been justified through faith, we have peace with God through our Lord Jesus Christ, through whom we have gained access by faith into this grace in which we now stand. And we boast in the hope of the glory of God." This verse emphasizes the foundational role of faith in justification and the resultant peace and hope believers have in Christ.

II. The Process of Sanctification:

Romans 6:4: "We were therefore buried with him through baptism into death in order that, just as Christ was raised from the dead through the glory of the Father, we too may live a new life." This passage illustrates the transformative nature of sanctification, where believers are united with Christ in His death and resurrection, experiencing newness of life.

2 Corinthians 3:18: "And we all, who with unveiled faces contemplate the Lord's glory, are being transformed into his image with ever-increasing glory, which comes from the Lord, who is the Spirit." This verse highlights the ongoing process of transformation into the likeness of Christ through the work of the Holy Spirit.

III. The Assurance of Glorification:

Romans 8:30: "And those he predestined, he also called; those he called, he also justified; those he justified, he also glorified." This verse provides believers with the assurance of their ultimate glorification, highlighting the unbroken chain of God's sovereign work in their lives.

1 John 3:2: "Dear friends, now we are children of God, and what we will be has not yet been made known. But we know that when Christ appears, we shall be like him, for we shall see him as he is." This passage reaffirms the believers' future glorification, where they will be fully transformed into the likeness of Christ upon His return.

IV. The Transformative Power of God's Word:

Hebrews 4:12: "For the word of God is alive and active. Sharper than any double-edged sword, it penetrates even to dividing soul and spirit, joints and marrow; it judges the thoughts and attitudes of the heart." This verse highlights the transformative power of God's Word in the believer's life, shaping their character and conforming them to the image of Christ.

Philippians 1:6: "Being confident of this, that he who began a good work in you will carry it on to completion until the day of Christ

Jesus." This passage assures believers of God's faithful work in their lives, ensuring that He will bring the process of sanctification to completion, leading to their glorification.

The journey of justification and glorification embodies the transformative work of God in redeeming and transforming His people. As believers navigate this journey, may they find assurance in God's unwavering promise of redemption and trust in His faithful work of sanctification. May they embrace the transformative power of God's Word and look forward with hope to the day of their ultimate glorification, when they will be fully conformed to the image of Christ.

God's Eternal Plan:

God's eternal plan for salvation stands as a testament to His unchanging purposes and faithfulness to fulfill His promises. From eternity past to eternity future, God has orchestrated every detail of His redemptive plan, ensuring the salvation of His people and the glorification of His name. Romans 8:28-30 unveils glimpses of this eternal plan, offering believers assurance in God's sovereign work and unwavering faithfulness. In this reflection, we explore the depths of God's eternal plan, finding assurance in His unchanging purposes and steadfast commitment to His people.

I. The Sovereignty of God's Plan:

Ephesians 1:11: "In him we were also chosen, having been predestined according to the plan of him who works out everything in conformity with the purpose of his will." This verse underscores the sovereignty of God's plan, highlighting His meticulous orchestration of every detail according to His will.

Isaiah 46:9-10: "Remember the former things, those of long ago; I am God, and there is no other; I am God, and there is none like me. I make known the end from the beginning, from ancient times, what is still to come. I say, 'My purpose will stand, and I will do all that I please.'" This passage reaffirms God's sovereignty over His eternal plan, declaring His ability to accomplish His purposes according to His will.

II. The Faithfulness of God's Promises:

2 Corinthians 1:20: "For no matter how many promises God has made, they are 'Yes' in Christ. And so through him the 'Amen' is spoken by us to the glory of God." This verse assures believers of the faithfulness of God's promises, emphasizing their fulfillment in Christ.

Hebrews 10:23: "Let us hold unswervingly to the hope we profess, for he who promised is faithful." This passage encourages believers to hold fast to the hope of God's promises, confident in His faithfulness to fulfill them.

III. The Unfolding of God's Plan:

Acts 2:23: "This man was handed over to you by God's deliberate plan and foreknowledge; and you, with the help of wicked men, put him to death by nailing him to the cross." This verse illustrates the deliberate unfolding of God's plan for salvation, culminating in the death and resurrection of Jesus Christ.

Ephesians 3:11: "According to his eternal purpose that he accomplished in Christ Jesus our Lord." This passage highlights the fulfillment of God's eternal purpose in Christ, underscoring His sovereign work of redemption through His Son.

IV. The Assurance of Believers:

Romans 8:28: "And we know that in all things God works for the good of those who love him, who have been called according to his purpose." This verse provides believers with assurance in God's sovereign work, assuring them that He works all things together for their ultimate good.

Philippians 1:6: "Being confident of this, that he who began a good work in you will carry it on to completion until the day of Christ Jesus." This passage reaffirms believers' confidence in God's faithfulness to fulfill His work of salvation and sanctification in their lives.

God's eternal plan for salvation stands as a testament to His sovereignty, faithfulness, and unchanging purposes. As believers navigate the journey of faith, may they find assurance in the steadfastness of God's promises and trust in His sovereign work to fulfill His eternal plan. May they rest in the assurance that God's purposes will stand, and He will accomplish all that He has promised for the glory of His name.

Romans 8:31-39:

As we approach the culmination of Romans 8, we encounter verses 31-39, where Paul delivers a resounding declaration of God's unfailing love and unshakable faithfulness towards His people. In these verses, we are invited to bask in the assurance of God's unbreakable covenant of love and to find solace in the overwhelming victory we have in Christ.

Paul begins by posing a rhetorical question, designed to elicit awe and wonder in the hearts of believers: "If God is for us, who can be against us?" With this question, Paul sets the stage for a triumphant affirmation of God's steadfast love and unwavering commitment to His people.

He goes on to enumerate the countless reasons why we can be confident in God's love and victorious in Christ. From His provision of His Son to His intercession on our behalf, Paul paints a portrait of a God who is actively engaged in the lives of His people, working tirelessly for their good and ultimate redemption.

But perhaps what is most striking about these verses is the depth of Paul's conviction regarding God's love. He declares with certainty that nothing—neither present sufferings nor future uncertainties, neither height nor depth nor anything else in all creation—can separate us from the love of God in Christ Jesus our Lord.

As we delve into these verses, let us be reminded of the unshakable foundation of God's love upon which we stand. Let us take comfort in the knowledge that we are more than conquerors through Him who loved us and that nothing can ever separate us from His love.

May this exploration of Romans 8:31-39 deepen our understanding of the immeasurable love of God and ignite within us a passion to live lives that are rooted and grounded in His love. And may it inspire us to walk in the confidence of our identity as beloved children of God, secure in the knowledge that nothing can ever separate us from His unfailing love.

The Unshakable Love Of God:

In the midst of life's uncertainties and trials, believers find solace and strength in the unshakable love of God. Romans 8:31-39 reassures us of the depth and constancy of God's affection, offering security and comfort in the knowledge of His steadfast love. In this reflection, we explore the profound assurance believers find in God's love, drawing from Scripture to illuminate its unwavering nature and transformative power.

1. God's Love: A Firm Foundation

Romans 8:38-39: "For I am convinced that neither death nor life, neither angels nor demons, neither the present nor the future, nor any powers, neither height nor depth, nor anything else in all creation, will be able to separate us from the love of God that is in Christ Jesus our Lord." These verses affirm the unbreakable bond of love between God and His people, transcending all circumstances and challenges.

1 John 4:16: "And so we know and rely on the love God has for us. God is love. Whoever lives in love lives in God, and God in them." This verse underscores the foundational truth that God's very nature is love, providing believers with a secure and unwavering anchor for their faith.

2. Security in God's Love

Psalm 91:14-15: "Because he loves me," says the Lord, "I will rescue him; I will protect him, for he acknowledges my name. He will call on me, and I will answer him; I will be with him in trouble, I will deliver him and honor him." These verses assure believers of God's protective presence and deliverance in times of trouble, rooted in His boundless love.

Jeremiah 31:3: "The Lord appeared to us in the past, saying: 'I have loved you with an everlasting love; I have drawn you with unfailing kindness.'" This passage speaks of God's everlasting love for His people, extending throughout eternity and encompassing every aspect of their lives.

3. Comfort in God's Love

Psalm 23:4: "Even though I walk through the darkest valley, I will fear no evil, for you are with me; your rod and your staff, they comfort me." These words from the psalmist illustrate the comfort and assurance believers find in the presence of God, knowing that His love surrounds them even in the darkest moments.

Isaiah 41:10: "So do not fear, for I am with you; do not be dismayed, for I am your God. I will strengthen you and help you; I will uphold you with my righteous right hand." This verse offers reassurance and encouragement to believers, reminding them of God's faithful presence and support in every circumstance.

The unshakable love of God stands as a source of assurance and comfort for believers, providing a firm foundation amidst life's uncertainties. As we meditate on the Scriptures and reflect on the depth of God's love, may we find security in His steadfast affection and draw strength from His unwavering presence in our lives.

Victory In Christ:

In the midst of life's trials and tribulations, believers find unyielding victory in Christ. Romans 8:31-39 assures us of our triumphant standing in Him, empowering us to overcome every obstacle and challenge through His overwhelming power and grace. In this reflection, we explore the reality of victory in Christ, drawing encouragement from Scripture to face life's challenges with confidence and faith.

1. The Assurance of Victory

Romans 8:37: "No, in all these things we are more than conquerors through him who loved us." This verse declares believers as more than conquerors through Christ's love, assuring us of victory over every trial and hardship we may face.

1 Corinthians 15:57: "But thanks be to God! He gives us the victory through our Lord Jesus Christ." This passage celebrates the victory that believers have in Christ, acknowledging God's role in granting triumph over sin and death.

2. Overcoming the World

John 16:33: "I have told you these things, so that in me you may have peace. In this world you will have trouble. But take heart! I have overcome the world." Jesus' words offer encouragement and assurance to believers, reminding us that He has overcome the world and empowers us to do the same.

1 John 5:4: "For everyone born of God overcomes the world. This is the victory that has overcome the world, even our faith." This verse emphasizes the role of faith in overcoming the world, affirming believers as victorious through their union with Christ.

3. Conquerors Through Christ

2 Corinthians 2:14: "But thanks be to God, who always leads us as captives in Christ's triumphal procession and uses us to spread the aroma of the knowledge of him everywhere." This imagery of triumphal procession underscores believers' victorious status in Christ, as we are led in His triumph over sin and death.

- Ephesians 6:10: "Finally, be strong in the Lord and in his mighty power." This exhortation from Ephesians encourages believers to draw strength from the Lord's mighty power, recognizing His role in enabling us to stand firm and victorious in spiritual battles.

Victory in Christ is not just a distant hope but a present reality for believers. As we face life's challenges, may we draw encouragement from His overwhelming power and grace, knowing that we are more than conquerors through Him who loves us. Let us stand firm in the assurance of victory, trusting in the One who has overcome the world on our behalf.

The Unbreakable Bond:

The bond between believers and God is unbreakable, rooted in His unfailing love and faithfulness. Romans 8:31-39 reassures us of the eternal security we have in our relationship with Him, providing assurance of His constant presence and unwavering support. In this reflection, we delve into the unbreakable bond between believers and God, drawing from Scripture to highlight the assurance of His unfailing presence and eternal security.

1. God's Promise of Presence

Deuteronomy 31:6: "Be strong and courageous. Do not be afraid or terrified because of them, for the Lord your God goes with you; he will never leave you nor forsake you." This promise from the Old Testament assures believers of God's constant presence and His commitment to never leave nor forsake them.

Hebrews 13:5: "Keep your lives free from the love of money and be content with what you have, because God has said, 'Never will I leave you; never will I forsake you.'" This New Testament affirmation echoes the assurance of God's presence, emphasizing His faithfulness to His people throughout all circumstances.

2. The Security of Believers

John 10:28-29: "I give them eternal life, and they shall never perish; no one will snatch them out of my hand. My Father, who has given them to me, is greater than all; no one can snatch them out of my Father's hand." Jesus' words affirm the eternal security of believers, assuring us that no one can separate us from His love and protection.

Romans 8:38-39: "For I am convinced that neither death nor life, neither angels nor demons, neither the present nor the future, nor any powers, neither height nor depth, nor anything else in all creation, will be able to separate us from the love of God that is in Christ Jesus our Lord." These verses underscore the inseparable bond between believers and God, highlighting the assurance of His unfailing love and presence.

3. The Covenant of Faithfulness

Psalm 89:33-34: "But I will not take my love from him, nor will I ever betray my faithfulness. I will not violate my covenant or alter what my lips have uttered." This psalmist's declaration reflects God's unchanging faithfulness to His covenant with His people, emphasizing His commitment to never revoke His love or faithfulness.

Isaiah 54:10: "Though the mountains be shaken and the hills be removed, yet my unfailing love for you will not be shaken nor my covenant of peace be removed," says the Lord, who has compassion on you." This prophetic assurance speaks of God's unfailing love and the unshakable nature of His covenant with His people, even in the face of adversity.

The bond between believers and God is unbreakable, rooted in His unfailing love and faithfulness. As we meditate on the Scriptures and reflect on the assurance of His unfailing presence and eternal security, may we find comfort and strength in knowing that nothing can separate us from His love. Let us rest in the assurance of His faithfulness, trusting in His promise to never leave nor forsake us, now and for all eternity.

Living Boldly In Faith

Fear and doubt often plague the hearts of believers, hindering them from living boldly and confidently in their faith. However, Romans 8:31-39 offers powerful truths that dispel these fears and doubts, empowering believers to stand firm in the assurance of God's love and faithfulness. In this reflection, we explore how the truths presented in these verses inspire believers to overcome fear and doubt, enabling them to live boldly and confidently in their walk with God.

1. Assurance of God's Sovereignty

Romans 8:31: "If God is for us, who can be against us?" This verse reminds believers of God's sovereignty and power, reassuring us that nothing and no one can stand against us when God is on our side.

Psalm 27:1: "The Lord is my light and my salvation—whom shall I fear? The Lord is the stronghold of my life—of whom shall I be afraid?"

This psalmist's declaration echoes the sentiment of Romans 8:31, affirming the security and protection believers find in God's presence.

2. Victory in Christ

Romans 8:37: "No, in all these things we are more than conquerors through him who loved us." This verse declares believers as conquerors through Christ's love, instilling confidence and courage to face any challenge or adversity.

1 John 5:4: "For everyone born of God overcomes the world. This is the victory that has overcome the world, even our faith." This passage reinforces the victorious nature of believers' faith, encouraging them to overcome fear and doubt through their trust in God.

3. Unshakable Love of God

Romans 8:38-39: "For I am convinced that neither death nor life, neither angels nor demons, neither the present nor the future, nor any powers, neither height nor depth, nor anything else in all creation, will be able to separate us from the love of God that is in Christ Jesus our Lord." These verses emphasize the unshakable love of God, providing believers with assurance and security in His steadfast affection.

Isaiah 41:10: "So do not fear, for I am with you; do not be dismayed, for I am your God. I will strengthen you and help you; I will uphold you with my righteous right hand." This verse offers comfort and strength to believers, reminding them of God's presence and support in times of fear and doubt.

The truths presented in Romans 8:31-39 dispel fear and doubt from the hearts of believers, empowering them to live boldly and confidently in their faith. As we meditate on these verses and reflect on the assurance of God's sovereignty, victory in Christ, and unshakable love, may we be strengthened to overcome fear and doubt, walking boldly in the assurance of His promises. Let us live courageously, trusting in the One who has overcome the world on our behalf.

Conquering In Hardship:

Hardships and trials are inevitable parts of life, but as believers, we are empowered by God's love and grace to conquer them. Romans 8:31-39 reminds us of the transformative power of God's love and grace, enabling us to find strength and perseverance in His promises. In this reflection, we explore how believers can conquer hardships and trials through God's love and grace, drawing inspiration from Scripture to navigate through life's challenges with confidence and resilience.

1. God's Promise of Strength

Isaiah 40:29: "He gives strength to the weary and increases the power of the weak." This verse assures believers of God's provision of strength in times of weakness, empowering them to persevere through hardships with His help.

2 Corinthians 12:9: "But he said to me, 'My grace is sufficient for you, for my power is made perfect in weakness.' Therefore I will boast all the more gladly about my weaknesses, so that Christ's power may rest on me." Paul's testimony highlights the sufficiency of God's grace in overcoming personal weaknesses and hardships, demonstrating the transformative power of His love and grace.

2. Perseverance in Tribulation

Romans 5:3-5: "Not only so, but we also glory in our sufferings, because we know that suffering produces perseverance; perseverance, character;

and character, hope. And hope does not put us to shame, because God's love has been poured out into our hearts through the Holy Spirit, who has been given to us." These verses reveal the redemptive nature of suffering, as believers find perseverance, character, and hope through God's love and grace.

James 1:12: "Blessed is the one who perseveres under trial because, having stood the test, that person will receive the crown of life that the Lord has promised to those who love him." This passage encourages believers to persevere under trial, knowing that God's promises await those who endure with faith.

3. Victory Through Christ

1 Corinthians 15:57: "But thanks be to God! He gives us the victory through our Lord Jesus Christ." This declaration celebrates the victory that believers have in Christ, affirming their ability to conquer hardships and trials through His power and grace.

Philippians 4:13: "I can do all this through him who gives me strength." Paul's testimony acknowledges the source of his strength in Christ, empowering believers to face any challenge with confidence in His enabling grace.

Believers can conquer hardships and trials through the transformative power of God's love and grace. As we meditate on Scripture and reflect on His promises, may we find strength and perseverance to endure, knowing that God's love empowers us to overcome every obstacle. Let us trust in His provision of strength and walk confidently in the assurance of victory through Christ, even in the midst of hardships and trials.

The Certainty Of Salvation:

The certainty of believers' salvation in Christ is a foundational truth that brings assurance and confidence in God's unchanging purpose. Romans 8:31-39 reaffirms the steadfastness of God's commitment to preserving His people until the end, offering believers unwavering assurance in their salvation. In this reflection, we delve into the certainty of salvation for believers, drawing from Scripture to highlight God's unchanging purpose and His faithful commitment to His people.

1. God's Unchanging Purpose

Hebrews 6:17-18: "Because God wanted to make the unchanging nature of his purpose very clear to the heirs of what was promised, he confirmed it with an oath. God did this so that, by two unchangeable things in which it is impossible for God to lie, we who have fled to take hold of the hope set before us may be greatly encouraged." This passage underscores the unchanging nature of God's purpose and His faithfulness to fulfill His promises, providing believers with unwavering assurance in their salvation.

Isaiah 46:10: "I make known the end from the beginning, from ancient times, what is still to come. I say, 'My purpose will stand, and I will do all that I please.'" This prophetic declaration emphasizes God's sovereignty and His ability to fulfill His purposes, ensuring the certainty of believers' salvation according to His eternal plan.

2. God's Faithful Commitment

Philippians 1:6: "Being confident of this, that he who began a good work in you will carry it on to completion until the day of Christ

Jesus." This assurance from Paul's letter to the Philippians highlights God's faithful commitment to believers, ensuring that He will bring to completion the work of salvation He has begun in them.

Jude 1:24-25: "To him who is able to keep you from stumbling and to present you before his glorious presence without fault and with great joy—to the only God our Savior be glory, majesty, power and authority, through Jesus Christ our Lord, before all ages, now and forevermore! Amen." This doxology celebrates God's ability to keep believers secure in their salvation, affirming His faithfulness to preserve them blameless until the day of Christ's return.

3. The Security of Believers

John 10:28: "I give them eternal life, and they shall never perish; no one will snatch them out of my hand." Jesus' words assure believers of the security of their salvation, emphasizing His ability to keep them safe and secure in His love.

Romans 8:38-39: "For I am convinced that neither death nor life, neither angels nor demons, neither the present nor the future, nor any powers, neither height nor depth, nor anything else in all creation, will be able to separate us from the love of God that is in Christ Jesus our Lord." These verses affirm the unbreakable bond between believers and God, providing assurance that nothing can separate them from His love and the salvation He has secured for them.

The certainty of believers' salvation in Christ is grounded in God's unchanging purpose and His faithful commitment to His people. As we meditate on Scripture and reflect on His promises, may we find unwavering assurance in the security of our salvation, knowing that God will preserve us until the end. Let us rest in the certainty of His love and trust in His unchanging purpose, confident that nothing can separate us from the salvation He has provided in Christ.

Nothing Can Separate:

The profound truth that nothing in all creation can separate believers from the love of God is a source of comfort and assurance in the Christian faith. Romans 8:31-39 magnifies the immensity and permanence of God's love for His children, offering unwavering assurance that nothing can sever the bond between believers and their Heavenly Father. In this reflection, we explore the depth of God's unfailing love and the reassurance it brings to believers, drawing from Scripture to underscore the permanence of His love amidst life's trials and challenges.

1. The Immeasurable Love of God

Romans 8:38-39: "For I am convinced that neither death nor life, neither angels nor demons, neither the present nor the future, nor any powers, neither height nor depth, nor anything else in all creation, will be able to separate us from the love of God that is in Christ Jesus our Lord." These verses encapsulate the immeasurable love of God, affirming its surpassing nature over every circumstance and entity in creation.

Ephesians 3:18-19: "may have power, together with all the Lord's holy people, to grasp how wide and long and high and deep is the love of Christ, and to know this love that surpasses knowledge—that you may be filled to the measure of all the fullness of God." This prayer of Paul emphasizes the incomprehensible dimensions of God's love, urging believers to grasp its vastness and be filled with the fullness of God.

2. The Permanence of God's Love

Jeremiah 31:3: "The Lord appeared to us in the past, saying: 'I have loved you with an everlasting love; I have drawn you with unfailing kindness.'" This declaration from the prophet Jeremiah echoes the eternal nature of God's love, affirming its permanence and unfailing kindness towards His people.

Romans 8:35: "Who shall separate us from the love of Christ? Shall trouble or hardship or persecution or famine or nakedness or danger or sword?" This rhetorical question posed by Paul underscores the unyielding nature of God's love, challenging believers to consider what could possibly separate them from His unfailing affection.

3. The Assurance of God's Presence

Deuteronomy 31:6: "Be strong and courageous. Do not be afraid or terrified because of them, for the Lord your God goes with you; he will never leave you nor forsake you." This promise given to the Israelites emphasizes God's enduring presence with His people, assuring them that He will never abandon nor forsake them.

Hebrews 13:5: "Keep your lives free from the love of money and be content with what you have, because God has said, 'Never will I leave you; never will I forsake you.'" This affirmation in the New Testament reaffirms God's promise of His continuous presence and love for His children, providing unwavering assurance amidst life's uncertainties.

The truth that nothing can separate believers from the love of God serves as a steadfast anchor in the storms of life, offering unwavering assurance and comfort. As we meditate on Scripture and reflect on the depth and permanence of God's love, may we find solace in His unchanging affection and trust in His faithful presence with us. Let us rest confidently in the assurance that nothing in all creation can ever separate us from the unfailing love of our Heavenly Father.

Embracing The Grace Uncovered

As we draw the final curtains on our journey through "Grace Uncovered," let us pause to reflect on the profound truths that have unfolded before us. Throughout this exploration, we have delved deep into the heart of God's grace—grace that knows no bounds, grace that transforms lives, grace that beckons us into intimate communion with our Creator.

At the core of our journey lies the timeless truth of salvation by grace alone through faith alone in Christ alone. We have seen how the gospel of grace stands as a beacon of hope in a world shrouded in darkness, offering the promise of redemption and reconciliation with God. It is through faith in Christ Jesus that we are justified, declared righteous in the eyes of God, and welcomed into His family as beloved children.

Central to our understanding of grace is the concept of identity in Christ. We have learned that our true worth and significance are found not in our achievements or accolades but in our relationship with Christ. In Him, we discover our true selves—redeemed, beloved, and chosen to fulfill His purposes in the world.

Our journey has also led us to contemplate the hope of future glory that awaits us as children of God. We have been reminded that our present sufferings are but temporary, overshadowed by the glory that is to be revealed in us. With eager anticipation, we await the day when we will be fully redeemed, our bodies transformed into the likeness of Christ, and creation itself liberated from its bondage to decay.

But perhaps most significantly, our exploration has unveiled the indispensable role of the indwelling Holy Spirit in the life of the believer. We have seen how the Spirit empowers us to live lives that are pleasing to God, guiding us in our journey of faith and interceding for us according to the will of God. It is through the Spirit that we experience the reality of God's presence in our lives, transforming us from the inside out and conforming us to the image of Christ.

As we come to the end of our journey, let us heed the call to embrace the grace uncovered—to believe in Christ Jesus with all our hearts, to trust in His finished work on the cross, and to surrender our lives fully to His lordship. May we walk in the freedom and victory that grace affords us, confident in the knowledge that we are loved, chosen, and destined for eternal glory in Him.

So let us embrace the grace uncovered and live lives that bear witness to the transformative power of God's grace. And may our journey of faith continue, guided by the Spirit, grounded in the truth of God's Word, and filled with the hope of the glory that is to come. Amen.

Prayer:

Now that you have known God's redemptive plan for you, and understand that you can't make yourself right with God on your own and by your own works, I know you have believed in the finished work of the cross. May I remind you that Christ gave up his life to die in your place. He exchanged your condemned status on the cross, and received the penalty that was due to you, so that you would not come to judgment(for he received judgment on your behalf).

If you believe the above paragraph as the truth, you are already saved from the penalty for sin and the power of sin too. The Spirit of God lives inside you from now on and you are a child of God henceforth. If still you feel like there is something to be done to make your salvation complete, read the following prayer(aloud or otherwise):

Lord Jesus Christ, thank you for dying o the cross instead of myself. Thank you for pulling all judgment to yourself, so that I may become the righteousness of God. I now believe you did so because of my frailty in the flesh, and that you reconciled me to God by the cross. I believe that you were raised up on the third day as a testament to your vindication and as a receipt for my salvation. Thank you for saving me and making me a child of God. Thank you for your Spirit, who bears witness that I am indeed a child of God, and helps me utter that you are lord. I declare that you are Lord! Jesus is Lord!

Amen!

Don't miss out!

Visit the website below and you can sign up to receive emails whenever Lawrence Muigai publishes a new book. There's no charge and no obligation.

https://books2read.com/r/B-A-NEDKB-OGXID

BOOKS2READ

Connecting independent readers to independent writers.

Did you love *Grace Uncovered: A Commentary on Romans 8*? Then you should read *Wisdom of the Sower*[1] by Lawrence Muigai!

[2]

Step into a world where resilience isn't just a word, but a way of life. In "Wisdom of the Sower," you'll find yourself at the crossroads of despair and determination, where the choice to give up seems tempting, yet there's a whisper of hope urging you to rise again.

Through these pages, I offer more than just words; I offer a roadmap to reclaiming your strength and rewriting your story. Discover the untapped depths of your own potential and unearth the courage to face life's challenges head-on.

This isn't just another self-help book; it's a beacon of inspiration, guiding you towards a life filled with purpose and passion. Dare to challenge the status quo and embrace the power within you. By the

---

1. https://books2read.com/u/3nM6pP

2. https://books2read.com/u/3nM6pP

time you reach the final chapter, you'll be equipped with the tools and mindset to conquer any obstacle that comes your way. Are you ready to embark on this transformative journey?

Also by Lawrence Muigai

Unmasking the Shadows
Unmasking the Shadows

Standalone
Grace Uncovered: A Commentary on Romans 8

Watch for more at https://greceandtruth.blogspot.com/.

About the Author

Embark on a journey through the labyrinth of my imagination, where words weave a tapestry of emotions and sentiments that resonate with the depths of the human soul. As an avid writer, I find solace in the rhythm of the written word, a melody that reverberates through the corridors of my mind and spills onto the pages of my creations.

Addicted to the intoxicating allure of storytelling, I immerse myself in worlds both real and imagined, exploring the nuances of human experience with a keen eye and a compassionate heart. From the tender embrace of love to the tumultuous depths of despair, my words serve as a vessel for the myriad emotions that course through the human spirit.

But beyond the confines of traditional storytelling, I find myself drawn to the boundless possibilities of the digital realm. As a seasoned blogger, I traverse the vast expanse of cyberspace, sharing my musings and insights with a global audience hungry for connection and understanding. Through the power of the internet, I bridge the gap between hearts and minds, forging connections that transcend the boundaries of time and space.

Yet, beneath the surface of my addiction to writing lies a wellspring of sentimentality, a deep well of emotions that infuse every word with meaning and purpose. For me, writing is more than just a creative outlet—it is a lifeline, a means of navigating the complexities of life and finding meaning in the chaos.

So join me on this journey through the labyrinth of my imagination, where every word is a stepping stone on the path to self-discovery and enlightenment. Together, let us explore the boundless possibilities of the written word and unlock the secrets of the human heart.

Read more at https://greceandtruth.blogspot.com/.

www.ingramcontent.com/pod-product-compliance
Lightning Source LLC
Chambersburg PA
CBHW071325140726

47996CB00005B/1826